the eggs & cheese
I love

JULES J. BOND

LEON AMIEL • PUBLISHER
NEW YORK

Basic metric conversions

Solid measures

15 grams	=	½ ounce
25 grams	=	1 ounce
50 grams	=	2 ounces
125 grams	=	4 ounces
225 grams	=	8 ounces
450 grams	=	1 pound
1 kilogram	=	2 pounds 2 ounces

Liquid measures

25 millilitres	=	1 fluid ounce
50 millilitres	=	2 fluid ounces
125 millilitres	=	4 fluid ounces
150 millilitres	=	5 fluid ounces
300 millilitres	=	10 fluid ounces
600 millilitres	=	1 pint
1 litre	=	1¾ pints

Published by
LEON AMIEL • PUBLISHER
NEW YORK
ISBN 0-8148-0698-8
©Copyright 1978 by Leon Amiel • Publisher
Printed in the United States of America

LIST OF COLOR PLATES

The publishers gratefully acknowledge the following sources for permission to reproduce the illustrations indicated:

American Egg Board: 17, 36, 71, 72, 92, 135, 136
Free Lance Photographers Guild: 74
House of Rufino Wines: 54
Moet & Chandron Wines: 53
Pickle Packers International: 110
Rice Council: 35
Spanish Green Olive Commission: 91

Eggs are the most versatile of foods and can be prepared in countless ways — they can provide whole meals — breakfast, lunch or dinner; meals for festive occasions or the simplest ones. They are the base for many sauces; most baking without eggs is nearly impossible — in short they are an essential ingredient in our lives. Most methods of cooking eggs are simple.

SOFT BOILED EGGS: Put egg in a saucepan, cover with cold water and bring to a boil. Reduce heat to simmering, cook for 2 or 3 minutes then remove egg.

CODDLED EGGS: Lower eggs carefully into rapidly boiling water, turn off the heat, cover the pan and let stand for 6 to 8 minutes, depending on the firmness of the eggs desired.

HARD BOILED EGGS: Put eggs in a pan, cover with cold water, bring to a boil. Reduce heat and simmer for 10 minutes. Remove eggs, cool immediately in cold water. To peel the eggs, crack the shells and peel them under cold running water. When eggs are too fresh they are more difficult to shell.

POACHED EGGS: Choose very fresh eggs. Poach only a few at a time. Use a heavy, rather flat saucepan. Add water and vinegar — 1 part vinegar to 5 parts water. Bring to just below the boiling point. The water should just barely simmer. Stir water in a swirling motion, break the egg and drop it into the center of the swirling water. This method will produce a fairly rounded poached egg with few "streamers". Cook for 3 minutes, remove carefully with a skimmer or slotted spoon, trim streamers off the eggs. If eggs are to be used immediately, keep them in a pan with warm, salted water until all are done, then remove them, drain on a towel and serve.

SCRAMBLED EGGS:

First method: Break eggs into a well buttered skillet, cook over low heat, stirring constantly. When eggs start to set, stir in a little heavy cream, remove from fire, stir in a little softened butter.

Second method: Beat the eggs lightly in a bowl. Pour them into the buttered top part of a double boiler, cook over simmer water stirring constantly. When the eggs start to set, stir in a few small pats of butter, and if desired, a little heavy cream.

OMELETTES:

There are a few basic rules. Omelettes take less than a minute to cook, so have all your utensils and ingredients ready. Have eggs at room temperature. Using cold eggs will often result in failure. Do not use too many eggs at a time. An omelette of three eggs is best. Never use an omelette pan for anything else but making an omelette. Never wash the pan with water. After a pan is seasoned, all it needs is to wipe it clean with a paper towel.

French omelette: Break three eggs in a bowl, season with salt and pepper. Blend with a fork but do not overbeat. Heat a tablespoon of butter in an omelette pan, pour the beaten eggs into the pan, stir the surface of the eggs with a fork, holding the fork parallel to the surface. At the same time, shake or tap the pan a few times to prevent eggs from sticking. Remove from fire. At this point put a filling on top of the omelette if desired. To fold the omelette, lift the pan at a 45 degree angle so that the still liquid part of the eggs runs to one side of the pan where it will solidify. At the same time slip the fork under the edge of the omelette near you and lift the edge. When the liquid egg is nearly solid, flip the edge over with the fork to make the correct fold.

To tilt the omelette out of the pan, hold a heated serving plate in your left hand. Hold the handle of the pan with your right hand, palm up, rest the edge of the pan on the edge of the plate. Now tilt both of them toward each other, in one motion flip the omelette into the serving plate.

To fill a cooked omelette, make it in the usual manner, slide it folded on a serving dish, shape it properly with a clean towel. Make a lengthwise cut in the center and push the sides apart slightly. Slide the stuffing into the omelette.

Egg Tips

Eggs should always be cooked slowly, whether scrambled, boiled or fried. Fast cooking toughens the egg white.

Don't beat whites in aluminum bowls or pans. Aluminum will darken them.

To remove a bit of yolk that slipped into the egg white, take a piece of egg shell and touch the yolk. It will adhere to the shell and can be lifted out easily.

When slicing hard boiled eggs, dip the knife blade in water, and the yolk won't crumble.

If you forget which eggs are hard boiled and which are raw, place them on a flat surface and spin them — raw eggs won't spin freely.

To prevent a cracked egg from bursting, add a little vinegar to the water the egg is to be boiled in.

Cold eggs crack often when put into boiling water. To prevent this, puncture the rounded end with a needle or pin.

When boiling eggs, bring them to room temperature after removing from refrigerator, or allow 2 extra minutes cooking time.

Egg Spreads

1.

2 hard boiled eggs
¼ cup mayonnaise
¹salt and pepper to taste

2 tbsp. grated onion
1 ½ tsp. anchovy paste

Rub eggs through a strainer. Blend with other ingredients.

2.

2 hard-boiled eggs
¼ cup mayonnaise
1 tsp. Dijon mustard

1 tsp. chopped capers
1 tsp. chopped chives
1 tsp. minced dill
salt and pepper to taste

Rub eggs through a strainer. Blend with other ingredients.

3.

2 hard-boiled eggs
¼ cup mayonnaise
½ tsp. chili powder

2 tbsp. minced green pepper
2 tbsp. canned pimiento, chopped
salt and pepper to taste

Rub eggs through a strainer. Combine with other ingredients.

4.

2 hard-boiled eggs
¼ cup mayonnaise
1 small clove garlic, crushed

3 tbsp. green olives, chopped
salt and pepper to taste

Rub eggs through a strainer. Mash garlic and salt to a paste. Combine eggs and all other ingredients, blend well.

Spread these mixtures on small rounds of toast or dark bread, garnish with a sprinkle of paprika, or a piece of pimiento or a slice of a stuffed olive.

Cheese and Egg Salad

(for 4 to 6)

½ lb. Gruyere cheese
6 hard-boiled eggs
½ cup sour cream
2 tsp. Dijon mustard

½ tsp. caraway seed, crushed
1 tsp. prepared horseradish
1 pinch of Cayenne pepper
salt and pepper to taste

Cut cheese into 1-inch cubes, chop eggs. Mix eggs, cheese and all other ingredients. Serve garnished with lettuce leaves, radishes and cherry tomatoes.

Cucumber and Egg Salad

(for 4 to 6)

3 medium cucumbers, peeled,
    coarsely shredded
4 hard-boiled eggs,
    sliced thin
1 large Bermuda onion,
    sliced thin

1 tbsp. dill, chopped
½ cup sour cream
salt and pepper to taste
1 tsp. sugar, or to taste
1 tbsp. parsley, minced

Gently combine all ingredients except parsley, put in a serving bowl, sprinkle with parsley and chill before serving.

Chopped Eggs

(about 1 cup)

6 hard-boiled eggs
½ cup minced onion
1 raw egg yolk
2 anchovy filets, mashed

salt and pepper to taste
3 tbsp. chicken fat or
softened butter

Chop the eggs very fine, blend with minced onions and the raw egg yolk. Combine and mix anchovy filets, salt, pepper, fat or butter, blend into the chopped eggs.

Chopped Mushrooms and Eggs

(for 6)

1 lb. firm fresh mushrooms,
sliced
1 tbsp. lemon juice
water
1 large onion, chopped
3 tbsp. butter

6 hard-boiled eggs
1 large clove garlic,
minced
salt and pepper to taste
1 tbsp. parsley, minced

Place mushrooms in a saucepan, add lemon juice and water to cover, bring to a boil and simmer covered for 10 minutes. Drain and reserve the mushrooms. Sauté onion in butter until golden brown, add garlic and sauté 1 minute longer. Chop or grind mushrooms, together with onion, garlic and eggs, add the butter the onions cooked in, blend in parsley, salt and pepper.

Eggs with Caviar

(for 2)

²/₃ cup heavy cream
2 tbsp. minced onion
2 hard-boiled eggs, sliced

3 tbsp. black lumpfish or
    red salmon caviar or other
4 thin slices toasted bread

Whip the cream until stiff. Blend in minced onion and caviar. Put the mixture in the middle of a serving dish, garnish with egg slices and toast.

Eggs with Shrimp

(for 4)

4 hard-boiled eggs, shelled
1 lb. cooked small shrimp
½ cup heavy cream

½ cup mayonnaise
salt and pepper to taste
2 tbsp. chives, minced

Cut the eggs in half, place them in the middle of a serving dish. Peel the shrimp and arrange around the eggs. Whip the cream until stiff, blend with mayonnaise, season with salt and pepper. Pour over eggs and shrimp, sprinkle with chives and serve.

Garlic Eggs

(for 6)

1 large clove garlic,
  crushed
3 anchovy filets,
  mashed
1 tsp. capers, chopped

1 tsp. chili powder
1 tsp. lemon juice
4 tbsp. olive oil
salt and pepper to taste
6 hard-boiled eggs

Combine all ingredients except eggs and blend well. Quarter the eggs, put them on lettuce leaves in a serving platter and coat with garlic sauce.

Pickled Eggs

(for 6)

12 to 18 small (pullet)
  eggs, hard-boiled, shelled
2 cups vinegar
1 cup water
1 tsp. pickling spice

1 tsp. salt
pepper to taste
2 tbsp. sugar
1 medium onion, sliced
  thin

Simmer all ingredients except eggs for half an hour. Pour over shelled eggs, cover and refrigerate for 3 to 4 days. Add beet juice to the marinade if you wish to color the eggs red.

These eggs are very good served with freshly grated horseradish.

Eggs in Aspic
(for 6)

6 eggs
1½ cups clear chicken
   broth or consommé
1 tbsp. (envelope) gelatin
   soaked in ¼ cup cold water

salt to taste
½ tsp. lemon juice
3 tbsp. Madeira wine
6 slices cooked ham
2 sprigs parsley

Boil eggs about 6 minutes, cool under cold running water and shell carefully, since the yolks are still somewhat soft. Heat chicken broth, add softened gelatin and stir until gelatin is completely dissolved. Add salt, lemon juice and Madeira, blend well and cool until the mixture is just starting to thicken. Use small ramekins or individual molds, pour aspic about ¼ deep into the ramekins and chill until almost set. Put a small piece of parsley in each ramekin, place one egg in each, spoon aspic on top to nearly fill the mold. Then cover with a slice of ham trimmed to the size of the ramekins, spoon a little more aspic over it and chill until well jelled. To unmold, dip each ramekin for just a second in hot water and then reverse onto a serving platter or dish.

Piquant Stuffed Eggs

(for 6)

6 hard boiled eggs
3 tbsp. Dijon mustard
salt and pepper to taste
½ cup whipped cream

1 tsp. minced shallots
3 scallions, minced
1 cup mayonnaise
paprika

Cut eggs lengthwise in half. Remove yolks. Rub yolks through a sieve, blend well with 2 tbsp. mustard, salt and pepper. Blend in whipped cream, shallots and minced scallions. Using a pastry bag with a star tube, fill the egg whites with the mixture. Blend mayonnaise with remaining 1 tablespoon mustard, coat the eggs with the mayonnaise, sprinkle with paprika.

Curried Devilled Eggs

(for 4 to 5)

12 hard-boiled eggs
(the smaller the better)
⅓ cup mayonnaise
1 tsp. curry powder (or,
if available, curry paste)

1 tsp. Dijon mustard
salt and pepper to taste
1 tsp. paprika
2 tbsp. minced parsley

Shell eggs and cut lengthwise in half. Remove yolks and rub through a strainer, then blend with all other ingredients. Fill the egg halves. The best and easiest way to fill them is using a pastry bag with a star tube. Garnish each egg half with a sprinkle of parsley and paprika.

Pate Stuffed Eggs

(for 6)

6 hard boiled eggs
1 small can liver pate
　(about 3 oz.) or a very
　good liver wurst
2 tbsp. minced shallots

1 tsp. lemon juice
3 tbsp. mayonnaise
salt and pepper to taste
capers
paprika

　　Shell eggs, cut lengthwise in half. Rub yolks through a strainer, blend with all other ingredients except paprika and capers. Fill the eggs with the mixture and garnish each half with a caper and a sprinkle of paprika. A pastry bag with a star tube will make the filling of the eggs very easy.

Casino Eggs

(for 8)

8 hard-boiled eggs
1 tbsp. Dijon mustard
1 tbsp. butter, softened
1 tbsp. mayonnaise
1 tbsp. sour cream

salt and pepper to taste
1 tsp. paprika
1 tbsp. grated onion
1 tsp. capers, drained, chopped
16 rolled anchovy filets

　　Shell eggs, cut in half lengthwise, remove yolks. Rub yolks through a strainer, blend well with all other ingredients except anchovies. Fill egg halves with the mixture, top each half with a rolled anchovy filet and serve.

Stuffed Eggs Surprise

(for 4)

4 hard-boiled eggs
1 tsp. Dijon mustard
4 tbsp. mayonnaise
½ tsp. capers, minced
1 anchovy filet, mashed
salt and pepper to taste

²/₃ cup Sauce Mornay
   (approx.) (p. 152)
¼ cup grated Parmesan
   cheese
1 tbsp. minced parsley

Cut eggs lengthwise in half. Mash yolks, blend with mustard, mayonnaise, capers, anchovy, salt and pepper. Stuff the halves and press them together to form whole eggs. Place one each in a buttered ramekin, cover with Mornay, sprinkle with Parmesan and brown in a 450⁰ oven. Sprinkle with parsley and serve.

Stuffed Eggs Vienna

(for 8)

8 hard-boiled eggs
1 hard roll, crust
   removed
½ cup milk
¹/₃ cup finely ground ham
4 tbsp. butter, softened

2 tbsp. sour cream
1 tbsp. grated onion
1 tsp. dill leaves, minced
1 tsp. Dijon mustard
½ tsp. paprika
salt and pepper to taste

Shell eggs, cut a cap off the narrow side and remove yolks carefully. Soak roll in milk, squeeze dry. Rub roll and egg yolks through a strainer, combine with all other ingredients and blend well until smooth. Fill the eggs and close with the sliced off cap.

Soy Eggs
(for 4)

4 eggs
½ cup Chinese soy sauce
½ cup chicken broth

6 tbsp. sugar
1 tbsp. grated onion
1 tbsp. sherry

Put eggs in a saucepan, cover with water and boil gently for 10 minutes. Remove from pan and cool under cold running water for 5 minutes. Shell carefully. Place eggs in a small saucepan, add all other ingredients and bring to a boil. Cover pan and simmer for 1 hour, turning the eggs several times during cooking so that they will color evenly. After one hour, remove pan from heat and cool eggs in their liquid for 30 minutes. Drain, quarter eggs, serve on a bed of lettuce leaves.

Tea Eggs
(for 4)

4 eggs
3 cups boiling water
2 tbsp. black tea

1 tbsp. salt
½ tsp. vinegar

Put eggs in a pan with cold water, bring to a boil and simmer for 10 minutes. Remove eggs from pan, cool under cold running water for 5 minutes. Then tap the ends of the eggs gently and roll them on a flat surface to crack the shells evenly. Do not remove the shells. Put 3 cups of boiling water in a small saucepan, add tea, salt, vinegar, put the eggs in the pan (the liquid should cover the eggs) and simmer for 1½ hours. Remove from heat and let stand in the liquid for 1 or 2 hours. Then remove them from pan, shell and serve quartered or halved as appetizer or garnish.

Devilled Eggs.

Fried Eggs Aumoniere

(for 4)

For the crépe batter:

¼ cup milk

2 tbsp. butter

½ tsp. salt

½ cup flour

2 eggs

¼ cup beer

For the dish:

4 slices of French bread

2 slices Swiss cheese

2 slices cooked ham

1 cup oil

2 tbsp. butter

4 eggs

Make the batter: Heat the milk to lukewarm. Melt butter, add salt. Put flour in a bowl, add eggs, milk and butter. Beat thoroughly and stir in beer. Let rest in the refrigerator for 2 hours.

Cut four 3-inch rounds from the bread, the cheese and the ham. Heat 2 tablespoons oil and all of the butter in a skillet and fry the bread rounds until golden on both sides. Remove bread, drain and keep warm. Fry the ham on both sides in the same skillet. Put a round of cheese on each round of fried bread, top with a piece of ham and keep hot.

In a very small skillet, heat the remaining oil. When it is very hot break an egg into it. Tilt the skillet so that the egg will be covered with oil on all sides, and with the help of a spatula push the white over the yolk. The egg, when fried, should be an oval the size of the bread rounds. Drain the egg on paper towels, quickly cook the rest of the eggs.

Make 4 crépes about 8 or 9 inches in diameter with the batter. Place them side by side on paper towel. Put in the center of each one of the bread rounds, top each with a fried egg. Tie up the crépes with string as if making a pouch. Put them in a buttered baking dish and brown them quickly under a broiler. Serve very hot.

Fried Eggs Aumoniere.

Deep Fried Stuffed Eggs
(for 4)

4 hard-boiled eggs
1 cup Ricotta cheese
2 tbsp. Parmesan cheese, grated
2 anchovy filets, mashed
1 tsp. grated onion

salt and pepper to taste
flour
2 eggs, lightly beaten
fine dry breadcrumbs
oil for deep frying

Cut eggs lengthwise in half, remove yolks. Rub yolks through a strainer, blend with Ricotta and Parmesan, anchovy, onion, salt and pepper. Fill the egg halves with this mixture and mound the mixture on each half to look like a whole egg. Roll each half in flour, dip in beaten egg and coat with breadcrumbs. Fry in deep oil until golden brown.

French Fried Eggs

Heat cooking oil in a deep skillet to about 375^0. The oil should be about 3 inches deep. Drop raw eggs, one at a time, into the hot oil. Turn them often with a slotted spoon or spatula to brown them on all sides. Fry for about 3 minutes. Remove with a slotted spoon and drain on paper towel. Sprinkle with salt and pepper when serving.

Scotch Eggs
(for 4)

1 lb. sausage meat	4 hard-boiled eggs
2 tbsp. Worcestershire sauce	1 egg, well beaten
1 tbsp. flour	1 tbsp. milk
pinch of salt and pepper	1 cup fine dry breadcrumbs
pinch of thyme	oil for deep frying

Blend the sausage meat, Worcestershire sauce, flour, salt, pepper, thyme. Divide the mixture in four. Roll out each of the four pats to a square, place one egg on each and roll the sausage mixture around it. Shape it with your hands to encase the eggs completely in the mixture.

Beat egg lightly with milk, coat the eggs with beaten egg, then roll them in breadcrumbs until they are well covered. Shake off excess crumbs.

Heat oil to 350^0 (or test with a cube of stale bread. When the temperature is right the bread will turn light brown in somewhat less than a minute.)

Lower the eggs into the hot oil. Fry for about 5 minutes until they are a deep golden brown. Remove with a slotted spoon and drain on paper towels. Serve at once. They can also be eaten cold, served with a salad.

Eggs in Bacon Nests
(for 4)

4 strips smoked bacon
2 tbsp. chili sauce
1 tbsp. A-1 sauce
4 eggs

salt and pepper to taste
4 tsp. melted butter
1 tsp. paprika
1 tbsp. grated onion

Sauté bacon lightly until transparent but not crisped or browned. Line the sides of 4 muffin tins with bacon, mix chili sauce and A-1 sauce and spoon a portion of the mixture into the bottom of each tin. Drop one egg carefully into each tin, season with salt and pepper, sprinkle with paprika and grated onion, spoon melted butter on top. Bake in a pre-heated 325° oven for about 10 minutes until set. Turn out on buttered toast and serve.

Grilled Eggs
(for 2)

4 slices firm white bread
3 tbsp. butter
4 eggs

salt to taste
Cayenne pepper to taste
½ cup grated Gruyere cheese

With a cookie cutter cut out 4 rounds of bread, 2½ inches in diameter. Fry the rounds in butter until light golden brown on both sides. Keep warm. Poach eggs, trim them neatly, place on bread rounds, season with salt and Cayenne pepper, cover thickly with grated cheese. Put under hot broiler, brown the surface quickly.

Egg and Gruyere Casserole

(for 4)

3 cups grated Gruyere
   cheese
3 tbsp. butter
1¼ cup dry white wine
1 tsp. chives, chopped
1 tsp. parsley, minced

1 scallion minced
1 tsp. minced shallots
salt and pepper to taste
dash of Tabasco sauce
6 eggs, separated

    Put all ingredients except eggs in a fireproof casserole, mix well and cook over a gentle flame, while stirring constantly, until the mixture is smooth and bubbly and all the cheese has melted. Whisk in the egg yolks until well blended, then blend in the stiffly beaten egg whites and cook while stirring, over the lowest possible flame until the mixture is well scrambled. Serve on hot toast triangles.

Egg Casserole
(for 6)

12 small pork link
  sausages
2 tbsp. Worcestershire sauce
2 tbsp. minced shallots
2 tbsp. minced parsley

6 eggs, separated
salt and pepper to taste
pinch of grated nutmeg
1 tsp. paprika

Put sausages and 1 tablespoon water in a small skillet, cover and cook gently for 15 minutes. Remove sausages and place 2 sausages in each of 6 ramekins or small gratin dishes. Sprinkle each with Worcestershire sauce, shallots and parsley. Separate eggs, being careful not to break the yolks. Beat egg whites stiff and season with salt, pepper and nutmeg. Spoon egg whites on top of sausages; with the back of a spoon make a depression in the center of each mound of egg whites, carefully put a yolk in the depression, sprinkle with paprika and bake at 350⁰ for about 15 minutes until yolks are set and whites nicely browned.

Cream Cheese and Eggs

(for 4)

5 eggs
8 oz. cream cheese
2 cups plain yoghurt
1 tbsp. chopped chives
¼ cup milk

4 tbsp. breadcrumbs
salt and pepper to taste
1 tbsp. butter
1 tbsp. minced parsley

Let cream cheese stand at room temperature until softened. Blend eggs, yoghurt, cream cheese until smooth; add chives, milk, breadcrumbs, salt and pepper, blend again. Spread mixture in a small buttered baking dish, bake at 350⁰ for about 30 minutes until set. Sprinkle with parsley and serve.

Eggs Boulangère

(for 4)

5 tbsp. butter
4 small baking potatoes
2 tbsp. butter
¼ cup grated Swiss
  cheese
¼ cup grated Parmesan
  cheese

8 eggs
salt and pepper to taste
pinch of grated nutmeg
¹/₃ cup light cream
  (approx.)
½ tsp. paprika

Peel potatoes, slice thinly, sauté in 5 tablespoons butter until soft and golden brown — turning them occasionally while sautéing.

Butter a baking dish with 2 tablespoons butter, cover the bottom with sautéed potatoes, sprinkle with grated cheeses. Break eggs carefully over the cheese, season with salt, pepper and nutmeg. Spoon cream over eggs, sprinkle with paprika and bake at 350⁰ for 10 to 12 minutes until eggs are set.

Baked Potatoes and Eggs

(for 4)

4 baking potatoes
¼ cup melted butter
4 eggs
salt and pepper to taste

4 tbsp. sour cream
1 tsp. paprika
1 tbsp. chopped parsley

Bake potatoes until they are done — 30 to 45 minutes, depending on size. Cut a slice lengthwise off each potato and scoop out the inside of the potatoes, leaving a ¾-inch thick shell. Brush the inside with melted butter. Carefully break an egg into each potato, season with salt and pepper, spoon a tablespoon of sour cream on top of each and sprinkle with a little paprika. Bake in 350⁰ oven for about 10 minutes until eggs are set and the top lightly browned. Sprinkle with parsley and serve.

Baked Eggs Italian Style
(for 4)

8 eggs
2 tbsp. butter
1½ cups tomato, peeled,
   seeded, chopped
2 tbsp. parsley, minced
1 tbsp. chives, chopped

salt and pepper to taste
4 Italian sausages (sweet
   or hot, according
   to taste)
3 tbsp. grated Romano cheese
paprika

Simmer sausages for a few minutes in water, then drain and fry until browned. Butter a shallow baking dish, cover the bottom with chopped tomatoes, sprinkle with parsley and chives, season with salt and pepper. Break eggs carefully on top of tomatoes, slice sausages lengthwise in half and arrange around eggs. Sprinkle with cheese and paprika, bake in pre-heated 375^0 oven for about 5 minutes until eggs are well set.

Baked Eggs Lorraine
(for 4)

2 tsp. butter
2 slices bacon, cut
   in half

4 eggs
salt and pepper to taste

Put ½ teaspoon butter in each of 4 individual baking or custard dishes. Put half a slice of bacon in each. Cook in a pre-heated 375° oven for about 5 minutes until bacon is transparent. Break an egg into each dish, season with salt and a good deal of pepper. Return to oven and bake for 5 minutes. Serve immediately.

Baked Eggs Provencale
(for 4)

2 tsp. butter
1 clove garlic, mashed
salt to taste

4 tbsp. tomato puree
2 tbsp. olive oil
4 eggs

Mash garlic with salt to a smooth paste. Combine with tomato purée and oil, blend well. Put ½ teaspoon butter in the bottom of 4 individual baking or custard dishes, add to each one-fourth of the tomato mixture; break an egg into each dish. Set the molds in a pan containing 1 inch of boiling water, bake in a 350° oven for about 10 minutes. Serve immediately.

Baked Eggs Lausanne
(for 3 to 4)

1 tbsp. butter
½ cup grated Swiss cheese
6 eggs
salt and pepper to taste

1 tbsp. minced onion
1 tbsp. minced parsley
1 tbsp. minced chives
2 tbsp. butter

Butter the bottom of a round baking dish with 1 tablespoon butter; sprinkle over it ⅓ cup grated cheese. Break the eggs carefully into the dish, keeping the yolks whole. Mix remaining cheese with all other ingredients except 2 tablespoons butter and sprinkle over the eggs. Dot with butter and bake at 350⁰ for about 10 to 12 minutes until top is nicely browned.

Baked Eggs Normand
(for 4)

2 tbsp. butter
4 slices cooked ham
    or Canadian bacon
4 thin slices Swiss cheese

8 eggs
salt and pepper to taste
⅓ cup heavy cream
1 tsp. paprika

Butter 4 ramekins or small baking dishes. Trim ham to size of the ramekins, put a slice in each. Top with a slice of cheese, trimmed to size. Break carefully two eggs into each ramekin, spoon a portion of the heavy cream over the eggs, season with salt and pepper. Bake at 350⁰ for 6 to 7 minutes, until the whites are well set but the yolks still soft. Sprinkle with paprika and serve.

Baked Eggs Surprise
(for 2 to 4)

4 large firm tomatoes
2 tbsp. oil
2 tbsp. butter
4 eggs
salt and pepper to taste

$^1/_3$ cup grated cheese
   (Parmesan or Swiss)
2 tbsp. minced chives
dash of Tabasco sauce
   (opt.)

Slice top off tomatoes, scoop out inside and discard. Place ½ tablespoon butter in each tomato, rub the outside with oil, place them in an oiled baking dish and bake in 350⁰ oven for about 10 to 12 minutes. Remove from oven, break one egg into each tomato, top with grated cheese, chives, salt and pepper and a dash of Tabasco sauce, if desired. Return to oven and cook for 10 minutes or until the eggs are set.

Swiss Baked Eggs
(for 4 to 6)

butter
¾ lb. Swiss cheese, sliced
8 eggs
salt and pepper to taste
$^2/_3$ cup heavy cream

2 tbsp. parsley, minced
1 tbsp. finely minced shallots
¼ cup grated Parmesan
   cheese

Butter the bottom of a baking dish, line with sliced cheese. Break eggs carefully into the dish, season with salt and pepper, sprinkle with parsley and shallots. Pour cream on eggs, sprinkle with Parmesan. Bake in 350⁰ oven for about 12 minutes until well set.

Piperade
(for 4)

¼ cup butter
¼ cup oil
1 medium onion, sliced
  very thin
1 green pepper, cut
  into thin strips
salt and pepper to taste

1 red sweet pepper,
  cut into strips (or
  ½ cup canned pimiento)
1 cup tomatoes, peeled,
  seeded, diced
4 anchovy filets, chopped
6 large eggs

Heat butter and oil in a heavy skillet, add onion and peppers, sauté gently for about 15 minutes. Stir several times, do not let brown. Add tomatoes, cook 5 minutes more. Beat eggs lightly, mix in anchovies, season with salt and pepper, and pour eggs into the skillet. Mix with the sautéed vegetables, cook until firm but still moist. Turn out on a serving dish.

Eggs Parma
(for 4)

8 eggs
4 slices Italian style
   ham (prosciutto or
   Canadian bacon)
4 tbsp. grated Parmesan cheese

3 tbsp. canned pimiento,
   cut in strips
3 tbsp. butter
salt and pepper to taste

Break the eggs in a buttered baking dish or small skillet; put the thinly sliced ham on top, sprinkle with salt, pepper, grated cheese; add strips of pimiento and pour melted butter over the eggs. Bake in 375^0 oven until eggs are set and cheese melted. Then put dish for a minute or less under a hot broiler until top is lightly browned.

Baked Eggs and Sour Cream
(for 4)

4 large egg yolks
½ cup sour cream
4 slices firm white bread,
   about 1-inch thick

3 tbsp. butter
salt and pepper to taste
1 tbsp. minced parsley
½ tsp. paprika

With a cookie cutter cut a round of about 3 inches out of each slice of bread. From the center of each round cut a smaller circle, leaving four bread rings. Heat the butter in a skillet, fry the four bread rings until golden brown on both sides. Place the rings in a buttered baking dish, carefully drop an egg yolk in the center of each ring, cover each yolk with sour cream, season with salt and pepper and bake at 350^0 for about 5 to 6 minutes until the yolks are set. Sprinkle with parsley and paprika just before serving.

Stuffed Eggs au Gratin
(for 6)

6 hard-boiled eggs
2 slices white bread,
   crust trimmed off
¼ cup milk
2 anchovy filets
2 tbsp. sour cream
salt to taste

½ tsp. paprika
1 tbsp. butter
1 cup sour cream
¼ cup flour
1 tbsp. melted butter
2 tbsp. grated Parmesan cheese
2 tbsp. fine breadcrumbs

Cut eggs lengthwise in half. Remove yolks. Soak bread in milk, squeeze dry. Rub yolks, bread and anchovy through a strainer, blend with sour cream, season with salt and paprika. Stuff egg whites with the mixture. Butter a baking dish, place stuffed eggs in the dish. Blend sour cream and flour, spoon over eggs, sprinkle with melted butter, grated cheese and breadcrumbs. Bake at 450⁰ for 5 minutes.

Creole Rice Omelette—See recipe on p. 60.

Scrambled Eggs
aux Herbes

(for 4)

8 eggs
½ cup sour cream
1½ tbsp. butter
1 tbsp. minced shallots
1 tsp. dill, chopped

1 tbsp. parsley, chopped
1 tsp. dried chervil,
   crumbled
salt and pepper to taste
paprika

Blend eggs and sour cream, add dill, parsley and chervil. Heat butter in a skillet, sauté shallots for 2 minutes, add egg mixture and scramble until done to your taste. Sprinkle with paprika and serve with toast fingers.

Note: Scrambled eggs should not be cooked in one minute over a blazing hot fire. Cook them gently, slowly — even in a double boiler. The result will be creamy and moist — not a rubbery mass streaked with white fibers.

Red Cherry Omelette—See recipe on p. 62.

Scrambled Eggs Acapulco

(for 2)

4 eggs
2 tbsp. heavy cream
1 tbsp. butter
1 sweet green pepper,
  seeded, minced
1 small ripe tomato,
  peeled, seeded, chopped

2 scallions, minced
2 tsp. chili powder
  (or to taste)
pinch of Cayenne pepper
¼ tsp. lemon juice
salt to taste
1 tbsp. parsley, minced

Beat eggs and cream lightly and set aside. Sauté green pepper in butter until soft, add all other ingredients except eggs and parsley, simmer for 2 or 3 minutes. Add eggs and scramble over gentle heat while stirring. Add parsley just before serving. The eggs should be quite creamy.

Scrambled Eggs and Smoked Oysters

(for 2)

1 tbsp. butter
4 eggs
2 tbsp. light cream

salt and pepper to taste
dash of Tabasco sauce
1 can smoked oysters

Beat eggs, blend with cream, salt, pepper and Tabasco. Heat butter in a skillet, add egg mixture and cook very slowly, stirring occasionally for about 4 to 5 minutes. Stir in oysters, heat through and serve on toast or buttered English muffins.

Scrambled Eggs and Oysters
(for 4)

3 tbsp. butter
3 anchovy filets
6 eggs
2 tbsp. milk
1 tbsp. parsley, minced

1 tsp. paprika
salt and pepper to taste
12 oysters, shucked,
   cut in half

Mash anchovy filets with butter. Break eggs into a bowl, add milk, parsley, paprika, salt and pepper and beat lightly. Heat anchovy butter in a skillet, pour in egg mixture. When eggs start to set, add oysters, stir and finish scrambling, soft or firm — to taste. Serve with buttered toast triangles.

Scrambled Baccala
(for 4)

1 cup dried shredded
   salt codfish
4 tbsp. butter
¾ cup milk, scalded
¼ cup light cream
1½ tbsp. grated onion

½ small clove garlic,
   minced
small pinch thyme
pepper to taste
6 eggs

Soak codfish in cold water for 1 hour. Drain well and squeeze out moisture. Heat butter in a skillet, add cod, sauté until light golden. Blend in milk, cream, onion, garlic, thyme and pepper, cook over gentle heat for 6 to 7 minutes, stirring often. Add eggs, cook and stir until scrambled but still soft. Serve on toast.

Mushrooms and Eggs
(for 4)

¾ lb. mushrooms, sliced
1 tsp. lemon juice
1 cup water
3 tbsp. minced onion

3 tbsp. butter
1 tbsp. chopped chives
salt and pepper to taste
4 large eggs

Place mushrooms, lemon juice and water in a skillet, cook gently until all water has evaporated. Remove mushrooms and reserve. Add butter and onions to skillet, sauté for 2 or 3 minutes until onions are beginning to take on color, return mushrooms to skillet, add chives, salt and pepper, add eggs, mix well and scramble until they are done to taste.

Eggs and Sausage
(for 4)

2 or 3 Spanish sausages
  (chorizos)
1 green pepper, seeded
  and diced

1 small onion, minced
1 tbsp. oil
4 eggs
salt to taste

Remove sausages from casing, break up the sausage meat, sauté in oil for 3 or 4 minutes, stirring occasionally. Then add pepper and onion and sauté 2 or 3 minutes longer, until vegetables are soft. Add lightly beaten eggs, salt; blend well with other ingredients in pan and scramble until done to taste.

Note: If Spanish sausages are not available, use sweet or hot Italian sausages instead.

Scrambled Eggs, Mushrooms and Peas

(for 4)

3 tbsp. butter
2 tbsp. minced onion
1 small clove garlic,
   minced
salt and pepper to taste

¾ lb. fresh mushrooms,
   sliced
1½ cups cooked green peas
6 eggs, lightly beaten
2 tbsp. grated Swiss cheese

Heat butter in a skillet, add onion and garlic and sauté gently until onion just starts to color. Add sliced mushrooms and sauté over low flame, stirring occasionally, until mushrooms are soft and most of the cooking liquid has been absorbed — about 10 minutes. Add peas, mix well, cook until peas are heated through, add eggs and scramble slowly until eggs are set. Sprinkle with cheese, season with salt and pepper, serve on toast.

Eggs in Avocado Sauce

(for 4)

2 tbsp. minced onions
2 tbsp. butter
¼ cup milk
1 tbsp. corn starch
2 ripe avocados

pinch of Cayenne pepper
salt and pepper to taste
8 eggs
1 tbsp. chopped parsley

Sauté onions in butter until soft and transparent. Dissolve corn-starch in milk, add to onions and stir until smooth and thickened. Peel avocados, rub them through a sieve and add to the onion mixture. Blend well, simmer and stir for a few minutes until the sauce is hot and smooth. Season with cayenne, salt and pepper.

While preparing the sauce, boil the eggs for 10 minutes, shell them and keep hot. When the sauce is ready, cut the eggs in quarters, arrange them on a serving dish and coat with the avocado sauce. Sprinkle with parsley and serve.

Eggs Cacciatore

(for 4)

4 tbsp. butter
2 medium tomatoes,
   sliced thick
4 chicken livers, halved
½ clove garlic, minced
   (opt.)

1½ tbsp. minced onion
salt and pepper to taste
½ tsp. basil
4 eggs
1 tsp. paprika
4 slices toast

Heat 2 tablespoons butter in a skillet, sauté tomatoes until browned on both sides. Remove and keep warm. Add chicken livers, onion and garlic to skillet, sauté until cooked, season with salt, pepper and basil. In another skillet, heat remaining butter, fry eggs to taste. Place tomato slices on each piece of toast, then add livers and the pan juices, top with an egg, sprinkle with paprika and serve.

Eggs Poached in Cream

(for 2)

4 eggs
¾ cup light cream
1½ tbsp. butter

1 tsp. grated onion
salt and pepper to taste

Heat cream and butter in a small saucepan, add onion, salt and pepper and bring to a simmer. Slip in the eggs, one at a time, reduce heat and cover. Simmer for about 4 minutes until eggs are done to taste. Remove eggs carefully, put in small serving bowls or ramekins, spoon cream over them and serve.

Eggs Benedict
(for 2)

4 eggs
2 English muffins, toasted
3 tbsp. butter

4 slices baked ham or
    Canadian bacon
Hollandaise sauce (see p. 155)

    Cut rounds of ham or bacon to fit on the muffin halves. Butter toasted muffins, cover each with a slice of ham or bacon and keep warm in a 250⁰ oven.

    Poach eggs for 5 minutes, remove from water with a slotted spoon, drain well and trim neatly. Put 1 egg on each muffin half, cover amply with hot Hollandaise sauce and serve immediately.

Poached Garlic Eggs
(for 4)

4 eggs
2 cups plain yoghurt
1 tsp. vinegar
1 large clove garlic,
    minced

salt and pepper to taste
3 tbsp. butter
1 tsp. paprika
pinch of Cayenne pepper
    (opt.)

    Put yoghurt in a bowl, beat until smooth. Crush garlic with a little salt to make a paste. Blend garlic, salt, pepper and vinegar into the yoghurt. Ladle yoghurt into 4 small serving bowls. Poach eggs, trim and place one egg in each bowl on top of yoghurt. Melt butter in a small pan, blend in cayenne and paprika and spoon some of this red butter over each egg. Serve immediately.

Eggs Benedict with Champagne Sauce

(for 6)

½ cup butter
½ cup flour
1 cup champagne
3 cups Half and Half
1 cup (4 oz.) grated
   Gruyere cheese

salt and pepper to taste
6 English muffins,
   split and toasted
12 thin slices Canadian
   bacon, sautéed in butter
12 poached eggs

In a saucepan melt butter and stir in flour. Gradually stir in champagne and Half and Half. Stir constantly over low heat until sauce bubbles and thickens. Add cheese and stir until sauce is smooth. Season with salt and pepper, remove from heat. Place muffin halves on serving plates, top each with a slice of Canadian bacon and a poached egg. Spoon sauce over eggs and serve.

Eggs Meuniere

(for 2)

4 eggs
6 tbsp. butter
2 tbsp. capers, well drained

½ tsp. lemon juice
3 tbsp. dry white wine
salt and pepper to taste

Poach the eggs to taste, drain well, trim and place on a hot serving dish. Melt butter in a small saucepan over medium heat until browned, while stirring constantly, whisk in capers, lemon juice, wine, salt and pepper. Pour piping hot over the eggs and serve.

Eggs Meurette

(for 4)

½ cup butter
½ lb. bacon, cut into
   narrow strips
1 medium onion, chopped
1 clove garlic, minced
2 whole cloves
2 cups dry red wine
½ cup chicken broth
½ tsp. sugar
salt and pepper to taste

bouquet garni (sprig of
   parsley, 1 bay leaf,
   pinch of thyme tied
   in cheesecloth bag)
4 slices firm white bread,
   crust trimmed off
8 eggs
1 tbsp. flour
1 tbsp. butter

    Heat 3 tablespoons butter in a casserole, add the bacon, onion and garlic, sauté until they are golden brown. Add cloves, wine, broth, sugar, salt, pepper and the bouquet garni. Simmer covered for half an hour.

    Fry the bread slices in butter, brown both sides, keep warm on a hot serving dish.

    Strain the sauce into a skillet, reserve the bacon strips. Bring the sauce to a boiling point, poach the eggs in the sauce, pushing the whites gently over the yolks with a spatula. Remove eggs with a slotted spoon, drain well, trim and place two eggs on each piece of fried bread. Combine 1 tablespoon flour and 1 tablespoon butter to a paste, add to simmering sauce and cook while stirring until the sauce thickens. Pour over eggs, top with bacon strips and serve.

Eggs Mornay

(for 4)

4 slices buttered toast
1 tbsp. butter
4 thick slices boiled ham
4 poached eggs

Sauce Mornay (p. 152)
½ tsp. paprika
dash of Tabasco sauce
(opt.)

Heat 1 tablespoon butter in a skillet, sauté ham gently, about 2 minutes on each side to heat through. Line broiler pan with aluminum foil, put toast in pan, cover each with a slice of ham and top carefully with a poached egg. Coat well with Sauce Mornay, broil for 1 or 2 minutes until nicely browned and very hot. Sprinkle with paprika and Tabasco and serve.

Poached Eggs Montero

(for 2)

1 cup Sauce Mornay
   (approx.) (p. 152)
4 rounds of toast
butter
4 slices cooked chicken
   breast
4 poached eggs

⅓ cup grated Parmesan
   cheese
salt and white pepper
   to taste
1 tsp. paprika
pinch of Cayenne pepper
watercress

Cover rounds of buttered toast with chicken, place a hot poached egg on top of each. Spoon Sauce Mornay over the eggs, season with salt and pepper. Sprinkle with Parmesan, paprika and Cayenne. Brown quickly under the broiler. Garnish with watercress.

47

Poached Eggs and Roquefort Cheese

(for 4)

4 small hard rolls
3 tbsp. butter
2 tbsp. grated Swiss cheese

3 tbsp. Roquefort cheese,
crumbled
4 poached eggs

Cut the rolls in half and remove the soft crumbs. Use 2 tablespoons butter to butter the hollowed-out rolls lightly, then sprinkle with grated Swiss cheese. Toast the rolls in a pre-heated 375⁰ oven for about 7 to 8 minutes until the interior of the rolls is golden brown.

Mix the Roquefort and the remaining butter, heat the mixture slightly in a skillet. Put the toasted rolls in a baking dish, fill each with a little of the Roquefort mixture and top each with a hot poached egg. Serve immediately.

Egg Foo Young
(for 4)

5 eggs
1½ tsp. salt
½ cup minced onion
1 small clove garlic,
   minced
½ cup bean sprouts,
   washed, patted dry

pepper to taste
3 scallions, chopped
½ cup minced celery
1 cup cooked pork or
   chicken, diced
2 tbsp. soy sauce
4 tbsp. oil

Beat eggs lightly with salt and pepper; mix meat with vegetables and soy sauce and blend well with eggs. Heat oil in a skillet or wok, and using a ladle or ¼ cup measure drop mixture, one portion at a time, into the oil. Fry each portion as you would a small omelette, brown on both sides. Remove each as it is cooked and keep warm.

Sauce for Egg Foo Young

¾ cup chicken broth
salt to taste
1 tbsp. sherry
1 tbsp. soy sauce

pinch of Cayenne pepper
½ tsp. sugar
2 tbsp. cornstarch
1½ tbsp. water

Blend all ingredients except cornstarch and water. Place in a sauce-pan and simmer for a few minutes. Dilute cornstarch with water, blend into the sauce and cook while stirring until thickened.

Steamed Eggs and Ham

(for 4)

1 cup chicken broth
½ cup minced cooked
  or smoked ham
2 scallions, minced
½ small clove garlic,
  minced

1 tbsp. sherry
¼ tsp. sugar
salt and pepper to taste
1 tsp. oil
5 eggs
1 tbsp. soy sauce

Heat broth until hot but not boiling. Blend ham, scallions, garlic, sherry, sugar, salt, pepper and oil. Beat eggs very lightly and blend gently with the ham mixture. Oil a shallow baking dish, pour in the egg mixture and cook in a steamer over boiling water for about 20 minutes until eggs have a custard-like consistency. After 15 minutes steaming, check with the point of a knife. If it comes out clean, the eggs are done. Sprinkle with soy sauce before serving.

Eggs a la Tripe
(for 6)

4 tbsp. butter
1 large onion, sliced
2 cups Bechamel Sauce
  (see p. 152)
6 hard-boiled eggs

½ cup heavy cream
pinch of dried thyme
1 tsp. celery salt
ground white pepper
  to taste

Melt butter in a saucepan, add onions, cover and cook very gently for 10 minutes. Do not let brown. Add Bechamel sauce, heavy cream, thyme, celery, salt and pepper, mix and simmer 10 minutes. Cut eggs in medium thick slices, add to the sauce and simmer 3 minutes longer. Serve on toast.

Ranchero Eggs
(for 4)

3 tbsp. oil
4 tortillas
1 tbsp. onion, minced
1 small clove garlic,
  minced
½ tsp. basil
½ tsp. marjoram
canned pimiento

1 tbsp. parsley, minced
½ tsp. ground coriander
salt and pepper to taste
1 cup canned tomato
  sauce
8 eggs, poached or
  fried
1 small avocado, sliced

Fry tortillas in oil, set aside and keep hot. Add onion and garlic to the same oil, sauté for a minute or so, add all other ingredients except eggs, avocado and pimiento. Blend and simmer for 2 minutes. Then place two cooked eggs on each tortilla, cover the eggs with sauce and top with slices of avocado and pimiento.

Note: Tortillas can be found in most markets in the section for Mexican foods.

Eggs Benedict with Champagne Sauce—See recipe on p. 45.

Spaghetti Carbonara

(for 4 to 6)

1 lb. spaghetti
½ cup butter
½ lb. bacon, chopped
2 cups smoked or cooked
  ham, diced
1 large onion, chopped
2 cloves garlic, chopped
½ lb. mushrooms, sliced

½ cup dry white
  wine
1 cup heavy cream
2 eggs, well beaten
¼ cup chopped parsley
salt to taste
⅓ cup grated Romano
  cheese

Melt butter in a large skillet, sauté bacon and ham until nicely browned. Add onion and garlic and sauté while stirring a few times for another 5 minutes. Add mushrooms, sauté 2 minutes longer. Stir in wine. Beat cream and eggs together until well blended. Stir into other ingredients cooking in the skillet. While the sauce is cooking, cook spaghetti *al dente*. Drain spaghetti and add to the sauce; add parsley, stir over low heat until well mixed, season with salt, sprinkle with grated cheese and serve piping hot.

Spaghetti Carbonara.

Camembert Soufflé

(for 3 to 4)

3 tbsp. butter
3 tbsp. flour
salt and pepper to taste
¾ cup milk
4 eggs, separated
2 egg whites

½ cup Camembert cheese
3 tbsp. grated Gruyere
 cheese
1 tsp. dry mustard
dash of Tabasco sauce

Butter soufflé dish (1-quart size) with 1 tablespoon butter, also a 3-inch paper collar to be tied around the dish. Melt remaining butter in a small saucepan. Remove from heat, blend in flour, salt, pepper and milk. Return to very low heat and cook while stirring until smooth and thickened. Rub Camembert through a strainer into the white sauce, stir until blended, then add, while stirring, Swiss cheese, mustard and Tabasco. Add egg yolks, one by one and blend until smooth, remove from heat and fold in stiffly beaten egg whites. Spoon mixture into the soufflé dish. Put dish in a pan, half filled with hot water and cook in 375⁰ oven for about 45 minutes, until well risen.

Camembert Omelette

(for 2 to 3)

6 eggs
2 tbsp. cream or milk
salt and pepper to taste

2 tbsp. butter
½ cup Camembert cheese
1 tbsp. chopped chives

Let cheese stay at room temperature until quite soft, scrape off the rind and measure half a cup.

Beat eggs, cream, salt and pepper lightly. Heat butter in an omelette pan, pour in eggs and cook until the bottom starts to color. Lift edges to let liquid egg flow in the bottom. When the top is still moist, add cheese, distribute quickly with a spatula or the back of a spoon, sprinkle with chives, fold omelette over and serve.

Cheese Omelette

(for 4)

5 eggs
1 tbsp. cold water
salt and pepper to taste
¼ cup grated Swiss
   cheese

1 tbsp. heavy cream
4 tbsp. tomato purée
salt and pepper to taste
1 tbsp. olive oil
1 tbsp. minced parsley

Combine tomato purée, salt, pepper, oil and parsley. Heat and simmer for a minute, keep warm.

Beat the eggs lightly with water, salt, pepper, blend in cream and grated cheese. Heat the butter in an omelette pan or skillet and cook the omelette in the usual manner. Slide it onto a hot serving dish, score the top with the point of a sharp knife and coat with the tomato sauce. Serve immediately.

Smoked Salmon Omelette
(for 4)

5 eggs
1 tbsp. cold water
salt and pepper to taste
2 tbsp. butter

4 thin slices smoked
  salmon
1 tbsp. capers, drained
¼ cup sour cream (opt.)

Beat eggs lightly with water, salt and pepper. Heat the butter in an omelette pan and cook the omelette in the usual manner. Just before folding place salmon on top, fold, sprinkle with capers and slide on a serving dish. Spoon sour cream on top if desired.

Chicken Liver Omelette Epicure
(for 4)

2 oz. fresh pork fat
4 tbsp. butter
$1/3$ lb. chicken livers
$1/4$ tsp. dried thyme
1 bay leaf

salt and pepper to taste
1 tbsp. minced shallots
$1/2$ cup port wine
9 eggs

Cut the pork fat into small dice and sauté them in a skillet in 1 tablespoon butter for about 3 minutes. Add the whole chicken livers, thyme, bay leaf, salt and pepper and sauté the livers over high heat until nicely browned. Sprinkle them with shallots, reduce heat and sauté 3 minutes longer. Pour in a strainer, discard pan juices and discard bay leaf. Reserve the livers and what remains of the shallots. Marinate the livers in port wine for 1 hour. Drain livers and cut them into thin slices.

Make two omelettes in the usual manner using the livers as filling. Serve immediately.

Creole Rice Omelette

(for 6)

Creole Sauce:

¼ cup minced onion
¼ cup slivered green pepper
2 tbsp. butter
salt and pepper to taste

1 can (8 oz.) tomato
   sauce
1½ cups hot cooked
   rice

Sauté onion and green pepper in butter until tender crisp. Add tomato sauce and seasonings; simmer 5 minutes. Stir in cooked rice.

Omelette:

6 eggs, beaten
¼ cup water
½ tsp. salt
1 tbsp. butter

3 slices (4" x 4") Swiss
   cheese
¼ cup stuffed olives,
   sliced

Combine eggs, water and salt. Melt butter in 10 inch skillet until hot. Pour in egg mixture. Stir rapidly with a fork until it begins to set. Smooth surface of eggs. Spoon on sauce; top with cheese. Continue cooking until just set and cheese melts. Garnish with sliced olives.

Acapulco Omelette

(for 3 to 4)

1 large ripe avocado
8 eggs
salt and pepper to taste

1 tbsp. oil
2 tbsp. butter

Peel the avocado, cut in half, remove the pit. Dice one half and cut the other half with a melon baller into small balls.

Beat the eggs, add salt and pepper to taste, blend in the diced avocado. Heat oil and butter in a skillet, add egg mixture and cook a flat omelette. Turn it over with a large spatula when the eggs start to set, finish cooking.

Place the omelette on a hot serving dish, garnish with avocado balls.

Red Cherry Omelette
(for 2)

¾ cup cherry pie
   filling
4 eggs, separated
¼ cup water

¼ tsp. salt
¼ tsp. cream of tartar or
   grated lemon peel
1 tbsp. butter

Warm pie filling while preparing omelette. Beat egg yolks until thick and lemon-colored, about 5 minutes. Add water, salt and cream of tartar to whites; beat until stiff but not dry, or just until whites no longer slip when bowl is tilted. Fold yolks into whites. On medium-high heat, heat butter in 10-inch omelette pan or skillet with ovenproof handle* until just hot enough to sizzle a drop of water. Pour in omelette mixture; level surface gently. Reduce heat to medium. Cook slowly until puffy and lightly browned on bottom, about 5 minutes. Lift omelette at edge to judge color. Bake in preheated 350⁰F, oven 10-12 minutes or until knife inserted halfway between center and outside edge comes out clean.

Note: To make handle ovenproof, wrap it with foil.

Bacon Omelette
au Gratin

(for 2)

4 slices of lean
    bacon
2 tbsp. butter
5 eggs
1 tbsp. water

salt and pepper to taste
½ cup Sauce Bechamel
    (p. 152)
1 tbsp. grated Swiss cheese
2 tbsp. melted butter

Cut the bacon in small dice, blanch them for 2 minutes in boiling water, then drain. Heat the butter in a skillet and cook the bacon until transparent. Beat the eggs with 1 tablespoon water, salt and pepper to taste, pour them over the bacon and make the omelette in the usual manner. Fold it when still very soft and slide it on a buttered baking dish. Coat the omelette with the hot Sauce Bechamel, sprinkle with grated cheese and brown it quickly under the broiler.

Eggs Capri

(for 3 to 4)

3 tbsp. olive oil
½ cup pitted, pimiento-
　stuffed olives, cut
　in half
1 small green pepper,
　seeded, diced
1 small clove garlic,
　minced
2 tbsp. grated onion

4 oz. Ricotta cheese
6 eggs
3 tbsp. light cream
salt and pepper to taste
small pinch of oregano
small pinch of crushed
　rosemary
½ cup grated Romano or
　Parmesan cheese

Heat oil in flameproof casserole or small baking dish, sauté olives, pepper, garlic and onion over gentle flame for 3 or 4 minutes until peppers are soft, add crumbled Ricotta and cook, stirring constantly for 2 minutes. Beat eggs lightly with cream, salt, pepper, oregano and rosemary, add to casserole and mix well. Cook over very low heat while stirring gently with a fork until the eggs start to set and are nearly done. Remove from fire, sprinkle with grated cheese and put under the broiler for 2 minutes until the cheese has melted and browned.

Spanish Omelette

(for 4)

4 tbsp. butter
1 medium onion, sliced
  thin
½ cup canned pimientos,
  chopped
1 small green pepper,
  seeded, diced small

1 large clove garlic,
  minced
1 tbsp. green olives,
  chopped
6 tbsp. olive oil
6 eggs
salt and pepper to taste

    Heat butter in a skillet, add onion, cook gently for 10 minutes. Do not let brown. Add garlic, pimiento, pepper and olives and simmer 2 minutes longer. Remove vegetables with a slotted spoon and keep warm. Beat eggs lightly, add salt, pepper, mix well. Heat oil in another skillet, add vegetables and sauté for a minute or two to heat through. Add eggs and stir constantly until they start to set. Then cook another minute without stirring, put a serving plate over the skillet and invert the flat omelette on the plate.

Baked Salami-Tomato Omelette

(for 4)

1 green pepper, seeded,
   chopped
1 medium onion, minced
2 tbsp. butter
2 ripe tomatoes, peeled,
   seeded, chopped

¼ lb. cooked salami,
   chopped
6 eggs, beaten
salt and pepper to taste
2 tbsp. minced parsley

Heat 1 tablespoon butter in a skillet, sauté pepper and onion for 5 minutes. Stir often, do not let brown. Add tomatoes and chopped salami, mix and sauté 2 minutes longer. Remove from fire, mix in beaten eggs, season with salt and pepper. Pour the mixture in a buttered baking dish and bake in 425⁰ oven until well set and the top is lightly browned — about 6 to 10 minutes. Cut in squares, sprinkle with parsley and serve.

Singapore Omelette

(for 4)

2 tbsp. oil
1 small onion, minced
1 clove garlic, minced
2 chili peppers (fresh
   or canned), sliced
   thin

6 eggs
1 tbsp. sherry
1 tbsp. soy sauce
pinch of powdered ginger
1 tsp. brown sugar
½ tsp. lime juice

Heat oil in a skillet, add onion, garlic and chilis, sauté gently until soft, but do not let brown; stir occasionally.

Blend eggs with all remaining ingredients, beat with a wire whisk until light and foamy. Add to skillet, cook over moderate heat until nearly set and the bottom browned. Put under the broiler for a minute or so to cook and brown top.

Smoked Fish Omelette

(for 3)

4 tbsp. butter
1 cup smoked fish,
    flaked (whitefish, cod,
    haddock or other)
½ cup + 1 tbsp. heavy cream
6 eggs, separated

3 tbsp. grated Parmesan
    cheese
salt and pepper to taste
1 tsp. paprika
1 tbsp. chopped chives

Heat 2 tablespoons butter in a skillet, add fish and 2 tablespoons cream, mix well and sauté for a minute. Remove from fire and cool.

Beat egg yolks with half the cheese, salt, pepper, paprika and chives until well blended, then blend in the fish mixture. Beat egg whites until stiff and fold in the yolk mixture. Heat remaining butter in a skillet or omelette pan, pour in egg mixture and cook over moderate heat for about 2 minutes until bottom of omelette sets. Sprinkle with remaining cheese and pour remaining cream over the omelette, place under a pre-heated broiler and broil for about half a minute until set and lightly browned. Serve at once.

Omelette Soufflé with Peppers

(for 4)

6 large red or green sweet peppers	5 eggs, separated
4 tbsp. olive oil	2 whole eggs
2 tbsp. butter	salt and pepper to taste

Brush the peppers with 2 tablespoons oil, put them in a preheated 500⁰ oven. Take them out when they are well scorched, rub off the scorched outer skin under running cold water. It will come off quite easily. Cut them lengthwise in half, remove seeds and membrane. Cut 2-inch diamonds out of each pepper half and cut the remaining parts into thin strips.

Heat butter and remaining oil in a skillet. Sauté the diamond-shaped pepper pieces until they are barely golden. Keep them flat by pressing them down with the back of a spoon. Take them out with a slotted spoon and reserve. Cook the thin pepper strips in the same skillet and reserve them separately.

Lightly beat together the 5 egg yolks and the 2 whole eggs. Beat the egg whites until stiff, fold them carefully into the beaten yolks, so that the mixture will be light and airy. Fold the pepper strips into the mixture. Reheat oil and butter in the skillet, adding a little more if necessary, pour the egg mixture into it. Cook the eggs on one side, turn them over with a wide spatula and let cook until golden on the other side, shaping them into the usual omelette shape.

Put the omelette on a hot serving dish, decorate with the diamond-shaped pieces of pepper, pour the pan juices over it and serve.

Cheese Soufflé

(for 4)

4 tbsp. butter
3 tbsp. flour
1 cup milk
salt to taste
pinch of Cayenne pepper
pinch of grated nutmeg

4 egg yolks
2 tbsp. heavy cream
½ lb. Swiss cheese,
   grated
6 egg whites, beaten
   stiff

Melt butter in a saucepan, add the flour and stir constantly over medium heat for 2 or 3 minutes. Then add the milk. Season with salt, Cayenne and nutmeg, stir with a whisk until the mixture is smooth and thick. Remove from heat and cool slightly.

Combine the egg yolks with the cream, beat them into the other mixture, then stir in grated cheese. Finally fold in the beaten egg whites. Butter and flour the bottom and sides of a soufflé dish, pour the mixture into it. Bake in 375⁰ oven for about 30 minutes. Serve immediately.

Soufflé Quiche Omelette.

Scrambled Eggs.

Salmon Soufflé
(for 4)

3 tbsp. butter
1½ cups canned salmon, drained, bones and skin removed
¼ cup light cream
¼ cup flour
1¼ cups hot milk
¼ cup Parmesan cheese, grated

¼ cup Swiss cheese, grated
salt and pepper to taste
1 tbsp. dill leaves
pinch of Cayenne pepper
pinch of nutmeg
4 eggs, separated
1 extra egg white

Place salmon and cream in a food processor or blender and process until smooth — or rub salmon through a strainer and blend well with cream. Heat 2 tablespoons butter in a saucepan, stir in flour and cook over very low heat, while stirring, until well blended. Gradually add milk while stirring, until blended and smooth. Simmer until thickened. Remove from fire, mix in salmon, cheeses, salt, pepper, dill, Cayenne and nutmeg.

When cool, beat in egg yolks using a wire whisk and beat until smooth. Fold in stiffly beaten egg whites. Pour mixture in a buttered soufflé dish, bake at 325° for about 35 minutes until soufflé has risen and is firm and browned.

Eggs Meurette—See recipe on p. 46.

Italian Omelette—See recipe on p. 76.

Italian Omelettes
Frittata

Frittatas have nothing in common with French omelettes, but the use of eggs. A frittata is never folded, it is perfectly flat and round, prepared over low heat and must be cooked on both sides. Unless one attempts to flip the frittata with a toss of the skillet, it is best to turn it over on a plate and slide it back into the pan, or to put the pan for a few seconds under a medium hot broiler to brown the top without having to turn the omelette. A frittata should never be deep brown, just golden in color.

Cheese Frittata
(for 4)

6 large eggs
salt and pepper to taste
1 tsp. paprika

¾ cup grated Parmesan
  cheese
4 tbsp. butter

Beat eggs until well blended, add salt, pepper, paprika and cheese and beat to blend well. Heat butter in a skillet until it starts to foam, but do not let brown. Add the eggs and turn the heat down to simmer. Cook for about 15 minutes or until the eggs have set but the surface is still slightly runny. Then either flip the frittata and finish cooking or put for about 15 seconds under the broiler until the surface is just set.

Asparagus Frittata

(for 4 to 6)

1 package (10 oz.) frozen
  chopped asparagus*
8 eggs
1 tbsp. grated onion
¾ tsp. salt

⅛ tsp. nutmeg
⅛ tsp. pepper
1 cup (4 oz.) shredded
  Swiss cheese
2 tbsp. butter

Cook asparagus according to package directions. Drain well. Beat together eggs and seasonings until well blended. Reserve ¼ cup cheese for topping, then stir remaining cheese and drained asparagus into egg mixture. Melt butter in large (10-12-inch) ovenproof skillet over medium heat. Pour in egg mixture. Cook until eggs are set, about 5 to 7 minutes. Sprinkle with reserved cheese. Broil about 6 inches from heat 2 to 3 minutes or until eggs are set. Loosen edges with spatula. Slide onto warm serving platter. Cut in wedges to serve.

*Substitute ½ pound fresh asparagus spears, chopped, if desired. Cook, covered in small amount of boiling salted water until tender, about 8 to 10 minutes. Drain well.

Frittata with Peppers and Sausage

(for 4)

2 tbsp. butter
½ cup sliced onion
¼ cup green peppers, chopped
1 large ripe tomato, peeled, seeded, chopped
2 anchovy filets, mashed
1 tbsp. green olives, chopped

2 tbsp. pimiento, chopped
1 tsp. basil
salt and pepper to taste
6 large eggs
3 tbsp. Parmesan cheese, grated
3 tbsp. butter
6 sweet Italian sausages, fried and fully cooked

Heat 2 tablespoons butter in a skillet, add onion and sauté until soft and light golden. Add green pepper, tomato, anchovy filets, olives and pimiento, basil, salt and pepper; blend well and simmer for 10 to 15 minutes, stirring occasionally. Remove from fire. Remove vegetables from pan with a slotted spoon and put in a bowl to cool. Beat eggs until well blended, add Parmesan, beat again and then blend in the vegetable mixture. Heat 3 tablespoons butter in a skillet and proceed to cook as in Cheese Frittata (p. 76). Garnish with sausages.

Italian Cheese Omelette
(for 4)

6 eggs
¾ lb. ricotta cheese
salt and pepper to taste
4 tbsp. butter

1 ½ tbsp. parsley, minced
1 tbsp. grated onion
¼ cup grated Parmesan
    cheese

Beat eggs lightly; cream ricotta cheese with a wooden spoon, blend with eggs, salt, pepper, parsley, onion and Parmesan cheese. Heat butter in a skillet, pour the mixture into the skillet, cook over moderate heat, lift sides of omelette with a spatula to let liquid parts flow to the bottom. Cook until bottom is nicely browned and top is set but still moist. Put for a few seconds under the broiler to brown top.

Onion and Tomato Frittata

(for 4)

3 large yellow onions,
  sliced thin
$1/3$ cup olive oil
1 cup canned plum
  tomatoes, drained, coarsely
  chopped
salt and pepper to taste

$1/2$ tbsp. anchovy paste
Cayenne pepper to taste
3 tbsp. grated Parmesan
  cheese
4 tbsp. fresh basil, chopped
3 tbsp. butter
6 eggs

Heat oil in a skillet, sauté onion slices until very soft and golden brown. Stir occasionally. Add tomatoes, salt and pepper, cook over gentle heat for about 10 minutes. Stir a few times. Drain off pan juices; cool and reserve the onion and tomato mixture.

Beat eggs with anchovy paste, Cayenne pepper; add tomatoes and onion, also cheese and basil. Blend well.

Heat butter in a large skillet, add eggs, turn heat very low. When the bottom of the eggs has set and the surface is barely runny (this will take about 10 to 15 minutes) put under the broiler for half a minute to cook the surface. Slide on a serving dish.

Meat and Potato Omelette

(for 6)

2 cups cooked meat, diced
3 large boiled potatoes, peeled, diced
1 large onion, sliced thin
4 tbsp. butter

1 small clove garlic, minced
salt and pepper to taste
pinch of thyme
pinch of grated nutmeg
½ tsp. paprika
6 eggs, lightly beaten

Sauté onions and garlic in 2 tablespoons butter until soft, add all other ingredients except remaining butter and eggs, and sauté until potatoes and meat are lightly browned. Remove from heat, cool slightly and mix with eggs. Heat remaining butter in a skillet, pour in the mixed ingredients and cook over moderate heat. As underpart of the omelette starts to set, lift with a spatula to let uncooked part flow underneath. When the underside of the omelette is browned, run for a few seconds under the broiler to brown the top.

Spanish Picnic Omelette
(for 6)

¼ cup finely chopped Spanish stuffed green olives
10 tbsp. butter
1 large round loaf unsliced French or Italian bread (about 10 inches in diameter)
½ cup chopped onions

¼ lb. mushrooms, finely chopped
¼ lb. boiled ham, chopped
1 large cooked potato, peeled, diced
½ cup sliced stuffed green olives
12 eggs, well beaten

Combine chopped olives and 2 tablespoons softened butter until well mixed. With sharp knife cut bread horizontally in half. With a spoon scoop out soft center of the bottom half of the bread leaving a 1-inch thick shell. (Save crumbs for another use.) Spread the scooped out surface of the shell and the cut surface of the upper half with the olive-butter mixture. Reassemble loaf, wrap in heavy duty aluminum foil and keep warm in a 300⁰ oven while preparing the omelette.

In a medium saucepan melt 2 tablespoons butter. Add onion and mushrooms, sauté until tender, 2 or 3 minutes. Stir in ham, potato and sliced olives. Cook, stirring occasionally, for 3 minutes.

Meanwhile, in a 10-inch skillet, melt 4 tablespoons butter. Pour in half the beaten eggs. Quickly add mushroom-ham mixture to cover eggs evenly. Pour in remaining eggs. As the edges begin to set, push egg mixture to center and shake pan vigorously to allow uncooked egg mixture to flow underneath. Cook omelette until top is just set but still moist — about 5 minutes, shaking pan constantly to keep omelette from sticking.

Invert a plate or rimless baking sheet over omelette. With one hand on the plate and the other on the pan handle, quickly invert pan, turning omelette out onto the plate. Melt remaining 2 tablespoons butter in skillet. Gently slide omelette back into the skillet. Cook until lightly browned on other side, about 2 minutes. Remove from heat.

Remove bread from oven. Unwrap foil and place bottom half of bread over top of omelette, quickly invert skillet turning omelette out into the loaf. Replace top of bread and serve.

Toast Nicoise
(for 6)

6 slices day-old good
   white bread
1/3 cup olive oil
2 cloves garlic, minced
pinch of thyme

6 tbsp. tomato paste
12 anchovy filets
2 tsp. capers, drained
6 slices Swiss cheese,
   1/8-inch thick

Trim crust off bread, heat oil in a skillet, add garlic and thyme and sauté bread slices until nicely browned on both sides. Remove bread, spread with tomato paste. Cut anchovy filets lengthwise in half and put 4 halves on each slice of bread, sprinkle with capers and cover each with a slice of cheese.

Place under broiler until well browned and bubbly.

Savory Cheddar Soup

(for 4)

2 tbsp. butter
1 large onion, chopped
2 tbsp. flour
1 cup chicken broth
3 cups milk
½ cup light cream
2 cups grated sharp
   Cheddar

1 cup grated Gruyere
   or Swiss cheese
salt and pepper to taste
1 tbsp. A-1 sauce
1 tsp. Dijon mustard
2 tsp. paprika
1 tbsp. parsley, chopped
dash of Tabasco sauce

Heat butter in a saucepan, add onion and sauté while stirring until light golden brown, about 10 minutes. Stir in flour and cook 2 minutes longer. Remove from fire, add chicken broth gradually, beating with a whisk until smooth, then blend in milk and cream. Return pan to stove, add cheeses and cook over gentle heat while stirring until cheeses have melted and the soup is smooth. Do not let boil. Blend in all other ingredients, correct seasoning, sprinkle with parsley and serve.

Cheddar Rarebit

(for 4)

2 cups sharp Cheddar
  cheese, diced
1 cup stale ale or
  beer
1 tsp. Worcestershire sauce
1 dash Tabasco sauce

2 anchovy filets,
  mashed (opt.)
1 tbsp. grated onion
1 tsp. lemon juice
4 egg yolks, lightly
  beaten

Place cheese, ale, Worcestershire sauce, Tabasco, anchovy, onion and lemon juice in the top of a double boiler or chafing dish. Cook over simmering water, while stirring constantly, until the cheese is melted and mixture well blended and smooth. Add egg yolks and continue stirring and cooking until the mixture has thickened. Serve piping hot on buttered toast.

Devilled Rarebit

(for 4)

2 tbsp. butter
¼ cup flour
1¼ cups milk
¾ cup tomato juice
2 cups sharp Cheddar
   cheese, grated (½ lb.)

1 large can devilled
   ham (4½ oz.)
1 tbsp. minced onion
1 clove garlic, minced
pinch Cayenne pepper
1 tbsp. soy sauce

Melt butter in a skillet or chafing dish over gentle heat, add flour and stir until smooth and bubbly. Add milk gradually while stirring and cook until smooth and thickened. Simmer very gently, stirring often, for about 15 minutes; add tomato juice, blend well, simmer for 5 minutes. Stir in all other ingredients and cook gently while stirring until cheese has melted and mixture is smooth and hot. Serve on toast.

Rarebit Epicure

(for 4 to 6)

1 lb. Swiss cheese, shredded
scant ²/₃ cup dry white wine
1 tbsp. butter
3 tbsp. minced onion
pinch of Cayenne pepper

2 tbsp. minced green pepper
½ cup fresh mushrooms, sliced
1 cup cooked shrimp or crabmeat, coarsely chopped or flaked

Sauté onion and pepper in butter until light golden brown, add mushrooms, sauté 2 or 3 minutes longer while stirring.

Put cheese in a saucepan or chafing dish, cook over gentle heat until cheese starts to melt, add wine and cook while stirring until smooth and well blended. Add all other ingredients, mix well and heat through. Serve on toast.

Scotch Woodcock

(for 2)

6 toast triangles or
  strips
butter
anchovy paste or
  6 anchovy filets

4 egg yolks
½ cup light cream
salt and pepper to taste
pinch of Cayenne pepper
2 tbsp. minced parsley

    Butter the toast and spread with anchovy paste or put an anchovy filet on each. Keep warm.

    Beat egg yolks lightly, blend with cream and put in top of a double boiler over simmering water. Add salt, pepper, Cayenne and parsley. Stir the mixture until thick and creamy. Spoon over pieces of toast, broil for a minute until top is browned.

Golden Buck

(for 4 to 6)

½ lb. sharp Cheddar
   cheese, shredded
½ cup ale
salt to taste

pinch of Cayenne
2 tbsp. grated onion
1 egg yolk
buttered toast

    Put ale and onion in a saucepan, add cheese, salt and Cayenne, melt over gentle heat stirring constantly with a wooden spoon until cheese is melted and the mixture is smooth and creamy. Blend in egg yolk, stir for another minute. Remove from fire, spoon over toast and serve.

Ham Rarebit

(for 2)

1 tbsp. butter
1 tbsp. flour
2 tbsp. light cream
¼ cup stale beer
  or ale
1 tsp. Dijon mustard
salt and pepper to taste
pinch of Cayenne pepper

1 cup sharp Cheddar
  cheese, grated
2 slices buttered toast
2 thick slices boiled ham,
  trimmed to fit the
  size of the toast
2 poached eggs

Heat butter in a saucepan, stir in flour and stir until bubbly; gradually add cream and beer, stirring until smooth and thickened. Blend in mustard, salt, pepper and Cayenne, simmer for 2 minutes. Add cheese and cook while stirring until cheese has melted and the mixture is hot. Place toast in a baking pan, coat with the cheese sauce, place a slice of ham on top and broil for 2 or 3 minutes until top is browned. Put on serving plates, place a hot poached egg on top of each slice and serve.

Spanish Picnic Omelette—See recipe on p. 82.

Whitstable Rarebit

(for 4)

1 pint shucked oysters
2 tbsp. butter
1 tsp. flour
¼ lb. Swiss cheese,
   shredded

pepper to taste
dash of Tabasco sauce
light cream
2 eggs, lightly beaten
2 tbsp. sherry

Simmer oysters in their liquor until edges curl and the oysters plump up. Drain, reserve oysters and the liquor.

Put butter and flour in the top of a double boiler and cook over simmering water until butter is melted and blended with the flour. Add cheese and cook while stirring until cheese is melted. Blend in pepper and Tabasco sauce. Add oyster liquor, stir and blend. Add some cream if the sauce is too thick. Blend in beaten eggs, stir for a minute; add oysters, sherry and salt if needed. Heat through and serve.

Asparagus Frittata—See recipe on p. 77.

Lobster Quiche

(for 4)

1 recipe paté brisée
(see Onion Tart p. 97)
1 lobster, 2 lbs.
4 whole eggs
2 extra egg yolks

1 tbsp. flour
2 cups heavy cream
salt and pepper to taste
pinch of grated nutmeg
2 tbsp. butter

Place the lobster in boiling water, boil for 8 to 9 minutes after the water starts to boil again. Drain and shell the lobster. Cut meat into small pieces. Roll out the pastry to about ⅛-inch thick. Line a 9-inch pie plate or flan ring placed on a baking sheet with the pastry. Arrange pieces of lobster on the pastry.

Beat together whole eggs, egg yolks, flour, heavy cream, season with salt, pepper and nutmeg. Blend well and pour the mixture over the lobster pieces. Top with butter. Bake at 350⁰ for about 35 minutes or until a knife inserted in the custard comes out clean.

Mushroom Quiche

(for 6)

1 recipe paté brisée
   (see Onion Tart, p. 97)
2 tbsp. butter
1 tbsp. minced shallots
1 lb. firm button
   mushrooms, sliced thin
1 tsp. lemon juice

salt and pepper to taste
½ tsp. grated nutmeg
1 tsp. Worcestershire sauce
½ cup light cream
4 eggs
½ cup grated Cheddar
   cheese

Heat butter in a skillet, add shallots, sauté for about 3 minutes until they are translucent and soft. Do not brown. Add mushrooms and lemon juice, sauté for 3 or 4 minutes over moderate heat until mushrooms are soft and most of the liquid has evaporated. Remove from fire, season with salt, pepper, nutmeg and Worcestershire sauce.

Beat eggs, cream and cheese in a bowl until well blended and smooth, then blend with the mushrooms.

Roll out paté brisée to ⅛ inch thick, line with it a 9-inch pie plate or flan ring placed on a baking sheet. Bake in a pre-heated 350⁰ oven for about 30 minutes until the quiche is well set.

"Quiche on Toast"
(for 4)

¼ lb. Gruyere (or
    Swiss cheese) grated
1 tbsp. butter
1 cup hot chicken
    broth
3 tbsp. grated onion

2 tbsp. chopped chives
2 tbsp. Sherry wine
salt and pepper to taste
4 eggs, lightly beaten
paprika
buttered toast

    Put cheese and butter in top of a double boiler over simmering water, stir until melted. Add all other ingredients except eggs and paprika, blend well and stir for a minute. Add eggs, blend and stir until the mixture is quite firm. Spoon on buttered toast, sprinkle with paprika and serve.

Onion Tart
Quiche
(for 6 to 8)

1 recipe pate brisée
  (see below)
4 large onions
3 tbsp. butter
1 cup heavy cream
1 cup milk

4 eggs
1 cup grated Swiss
  cheese
salt and pepper to taste
½ cup fine white
  breadcrumbs

Sauté onions in butter over low heat until they are soft. Do not let brown. Beat cream, milk, eggs and grated cheese until well blended. Season with salt and pepper. Roll out the paté brisée to ⅛ inch thick, line with it a 9-inch pie plate or flan ring placed on a baking sheet. Spread the onions on the pastry and pour egg mixture over onions. Sprinkle with breadcrumbs. Bake in a pre-heated 350⁰ oven for about 30 minutes. Serve immediately.

Paté Brisée

2 cups sifted
  all-purpose flour
1 egg

½ tsp. salt
3 tbsp. heavy cream
⅔ cup butter

Make a well in the center of the flour, put the whole egg, salt, cream and butter into it. Gradually blend the flour into the other ingredients. Knead until the dough is smooth. Chill for 2 hours before rolling out.

Leek Tart

(for 6 to 8)

1 recipe paté brisée
(see Onion Tart, p. 97)
4 large leeks
3 tbsp. butter
1 cup heavy cream

4 eggs
salt and pepper to taste
pinch of grated nutmeg
½ cup fine dry
    breadcrumbs

Trim off roots and the green parts of the leeks and discard. Split the white stems lengthwise and wash them well under running water. Cut them in thin slices. Blanch the leeks in boiling water for 5 minutes. Drain, rinse with cold water and drain again. Heat butter in a saucepan and sauté leeks until they are soft. Do not let brown.

Beat together cream and eggs, season with salt, pepper and nutmeg. Roll out pastry to ⅛ inch thickness, line with it a 9-inch pie plate or a flan ring placed on a baking sheet. Spread the leeks in the tart, cover with the egg mixture and sprinkle with breadcrumbs. Bake in a preheated 350⁰ oven for about 30 minutes or until a knife inserted in the custard comes out clean.

Swiss Fondue
(for 4)

1 garlic clove
½ lb. Gruyere cheese,
  shredded or diced
½ lb. Swiss cheese,
  shredded
3 tbsp. flour or
  1½ tbsp. cornstarch

2 cups dry white
  wine
1 tsp. lemon juice
pinch of Cayenne pepper
ground white pepper
  to taste
3 tbsp. Kirsch brandy

Rub the inside of a casserole or chafing dish with garlic. Put the cheeses into the chafing dish, mix with flour or cornstarch. Add wine and lemon juice, season with Cayenne and white pepper. Simmer over low heat, stirring, until the cheeses have melted. Stir in the Kirsch. Transfer the chafing dish to the burner of the dish or of a fondue set, and keep bubbling.

Regulate the heat so that the fondue keeps hot without boiling, or the cheese will become stringy. Serve with Italian or French bread cut into bite-sized cubes.

To eat, spear a piece of bread with a long-handled fondue fork, (or a skewer), dip into the fondue with a stirring motion until it is thoroughly coated with cheese. Serve with the same wine used in the fondue.

Shrimp Fondue
(for 4)

¾ cup grated Swiss
cheese
¼ cup grated sharp
Cheddar
1 tbsp. flour
½ cup dry white wine
1 tsp. Worcestershire sauce

dash of Tabasco sauce
salt to taste
1 tbsp. minced parsley
1 tbsp. minced chives
1 lb. small shrimp, cooked
shelled and deveined

Put cheeses in the top of a double boiler or the insert pan of a chafing dish and place over simmering water. Stir and cook until cheeses have melted. Dissolve flour in ¼ cup white wine, blend into the melted cheese and stir until smooth. Add rest of the wine, Worcestershire sauce, Tabasco, salt, parsley and chives and cook while stirring until smooth. Add shrimp and cook until hot. Serve with French bread.

Beer Fondue

(for 2)

1¹/₃ cups beer
¼ lb. Gruyere or Swiss
   cheese, diced very small
1 tbsp. tomato paste

pinch of Cayenne pepper
1½ tsp. Kirsch brandy
1 tsp. cornstarch
French bread, cubed

Bring beer to the boiling point in a saucepan, let it reduce by two thirds. Add the cheese, tomato paste and Cayenne, cook over lowest possible heat until the cheese has melted, thickened and is smooth. Blend together Kirsch and cornstarch, add to the Fondue, cook while stirring for a minute. Then transfer Fondue to a chafing dish burner and eat in usual way, dipping bread cubes into the Fondue.

Fondue Sandwiches

(for 2)

1 tbsp. oil
3 thin slices bacon,
  diced
2 oz. cream cheese
pinch of Cayenne pepper

¼ lb. Swiss cheese,
  shredded
4 slices toasted white
  bread, crust removed

Heat the oil in a small saucepan, add bacon and cook gently until the bacon is transparent but not crisp. Add cream cheese, Swiss cheese and Cayenne pepper. Cook over low heat, stirring constantly until the mixture is smooth and thick.

Put the toast in a shallow baking dish, top the slices with the cheese mixture, put under a hot broiler until bubbly. Serve immediately.

Raclette
(for 4)

Raclette is a traditional Swiss cheese dish — not dunked like a Fondue, but prepared in front of a fireplace. A big piece of Valais, a semi-soft cheese, is put on a wooden board or platter, set in front and close to the fire, and each person scrapes off the melted cheese onto his plate. Served with the Raclette are boiled potatoes, onions, pickles and usually a white Valais wine.

The following is an approximation — a substitute Raclette:

4 slices Muenster or Caraway cheese, cut in half
12 new potatoes, boiled in their jackets
12 sour gherkins or pickles

On each of 4 ovenproof plates, overlap 2 halves of cheese, place in 400° oven for 5 minutes or until cheese bubbles. Arrange potatoes and pickles on plates with cheese. Serve immediately.

Note: If desired, sprinkle cheese with freshly ground pepper before baking.

Blue Cheese Spread

(about 1½ cups)

6 oz. cream cheese
½ cup blue cheese
¼ cup creamed cottage
cheese
2 tbsp. brandy

1 tbsp. minced parsley
1 tbsp. grated onion
1 tbsp. soy sauce
salt to taste

Blend all ingredients until mixture is uniform and smooth (or put all ingredients in a food processor and process for a few seconds). Chill for at least a few hours before serving.

Creamed Camembert Spread

(for 4)

6 oz. Camembert cheese
¼ cup dry white wine
white pepper to taste

2 tbsp. butter, softened
1 tsp. minced parsley

Pare the rind off the cheese and discard. Put the cheese in a bowl, spread it out with a spoon to cover the bottom of the bowl, cover with wine and let stand for 12 hours or more, at room temperature. Then pour off any wine that was not absorbed, blend well with pepper and butter until smooth. Shape the spread into a round cake, put on a serving dish, sprinkle with parsley and refrigerate it just long enough — a half hour or so — to firm it up a bit.

Cheddar Cheese Spread

1 cup grated sharp
   Cheddar
1 cup farmer cheese,
   rubbed through a strainer
2 tbsp. prepared horseradish
3 anchovy filets, mashed

3 tbsp. minced onion
2 tbsp. pimiento, chopped
4 tbsp. mayonnaise
2 tbsp. sour cream
pepper to taste

Blend all ingredients until smooth. Let stand for a few hours before serving.

Cooked Cheese Spread

(about 3 cups)

1 lb. Gruyere cheese,
   grated
3 tbsp. butter
$\frac{1}{3}$ cup dry white wine

$\frac{1}{3}$ cup water
1 tsp. shallots, minced
1 clove garlic, minced
salt and pepper to taste

Place all ingredients in a saucepan. Cook over low heat, stirring constantly until cheese is melted and the mixture is smooth and creamy. Pour mixture in a crock, cool and let stand for a day before using.

Tangy Cream Cheese Cucumber Spread

6 oz. cream cheese
1 medium cucumber
salt and pepper to taste
3 tbsp. grated onion

1½ tbsp. prepared horseradish
(or to taste)
1 tsp. paprika
½ cup mayonnaise (approx.)

Rub cream cheese through a strainer into a bowl. Peel and grate cucumber, put in cheesecloth bag and press out the juice. Blend grated cucumber with cream cheese, salt, pepper, onion, horseradish and paprika. Add enough mayonnaise to give the mixture the right consistency for easy spreading.

Cheddar and Herb Spread

2 cups grated Cheddar
  cheese (White Vermont
  preferred)
4 tbsp. heavy cream
2 tbsp. sherry wine
1 tbsp. Cognac
3 tbsp. butter
2 tsp. chives, minced

2 tsp. minced parsley
pinch of rosemary,
  crushed
pinch of thyme
1 tsp. dried tarragon, crushed
salt and pepper to taste
pinch of mace

Put cheese in top of a double boiler, melt over simmering water, add all other ingredients and blend well with a whisk until smooth. Put in crocks, cover and refrigerate for a day or two before using.

Gouda Spread

1 1-lb. round Gouda
  cheese
$\frac{1}{3}$ cup beer

1 tbsp. A-1 sauce
dash of Tabasco sauce
$\frac{1}{2}$ tsp. crushed caraway seed

Cut a cap off the cheese, peel red wax off the cap. Scoop out the cheese, leaving red wax covering undisturbed and leave a shell about $\frac{1}{4}$-inch thick. Refrigerate the shell and leave the scooped out cheese and the cap at room temperature for a few hours. When softened, mash the cheese or process in a food processor for a few seconds, blend well with all other ingredients. Fill the empty shell and mound the top. Cover with foil or plastic wrap and refrigerate for a few days to improve the flavor. Before serving let come to room temperature, serve with rye or pumpernickel bread.

Swiss Fondue—See recipe on p. 99.

Gorgonzola Cheese Spread

(about 2 cups)

8 oz. Gorgonzola cheese,
cut in pieces
4 oz. Camembert cheese,
cut in pieces
1½ tbsp. grated onion

½ lb. sweet butter,
cut in pieces
¼ cup brandy
coarsely ground black
pepper, to taste

Let cheeses and butter come to room temperature, place all ingredients in a food processor and process until the spread is smooth.

If no processor is available, rub cheeses and butter through a strainer, then add all other ingredients and cream by hand until smooth.

Serve on dark bread or toast — or spread on bread and broil quickly — a half minute or a minute until melting and lightly browned.

Raclette—See recipe on p. 103.

Greek Cheese Dip

(about 1 cup)

1 cup feta cheese
2 tbsp. milk
2 tbsp. olive oil

pepper to taste
¾ cup chopped parsley
4 tbsp. chopped dill

Rinse cheese with cold water, drain and crumble. Place cheese in a food processor or blender, add milk, oil, pepper and some of the parsley and dill. Process or blend for a few seconds, add remaining herbs, blend until smooth. Add a little more milk if the mixture is too stiff.

Serve as a dip with raw vegetables, or with crackers, or put some of the mixture on small slices of ham and roll up in cigarette shape.

Lipto Cheese Spread

½ lb. cream cheese
2 tsp. paprika
1½ tsp. prepared mustard
1 small onion, grated

3 anchovy filets, mashed
½ tsp. caraway seed, crushed
1½ tsp. capers, drained, chopped
¼ cup beer

Rub the cheese through a strainer and blend well with all other ingredients. Let stand for a few hours or overnight before serving. Serve on squares of rye or pumpernickel bread.

Note: If a somewhat sharper flavor is desired, increase the amount of anchovy, onion and mustard.

Wisconsin Cheese Spread

(about 3 cups)

¾ lb. Cheddar cheese
¼ lb. blue cheese
3 tbsp. butter
1 tbsp. grated onion
1 tsp. caraway seed, crushed

1 tsp. lemon juice
1 tbsp. prepared mustard
1 tsp. paprika
salt and pepper to taste
½ to ¾ cup beer

Shred or grate the Cheddar cheese, put in a bowl, add crumbled blue cheese, butter, onion, caraway seed, lemon juice, mustard and paprika, salt and pepper. Blend and beat until well mixed and creamy. Add beer and beat until smooth. Let stand for at least 24 hours before using.

When using a food processor, add all ingredients at one time, process for a few seconds until creamy and well blended.

Cheese Balls

1¾ cups flour
1½ cups Edam cheese,
   grated
salt and pepper to taste

10 tbsp. butter
3 egg yolks, lightly beaten
½ tsp. powdered or crushed
   caraway seed

Sift flour into a bowl, add cheese, salt and pepper, mix lightly. Cut in butter and work the mixture until it has the consistency of coarse meal. Mix in egg yolks. Knead mixture on a floured board until dough is smooth and elastic. Shape dough in a ball, wrap in wax paper and refrigerate for a few hours. Then shape the dough in balls of about ½-inch diameter. Place on a buttered baking sheet and bake at 375° for about 15 minutes until the cheese balls are golden brown.

Cheese Biscuits I

(makes 14 biscuits)

2 cups sifted flour
2 tsp. baking powder
¼ tsp. baking soda
1 tsp. salt

¼ cup shortening
½ cup sharp Cheddar
    cheese, shredded
¼ cup buttermilk

Sift dry ingredients together and cut in shortening. Add cheese and buttermilk to make a soft dough. Knead lightly on floured surface for a few seconds, using as little flour as possible. Roll ½ inch thick and cut with a floured 2-inch cutter. Place on baking sheet and bake at 450⁰ for about 12 minutes.

Cheese Biscuits II

1 cup flour
1 cup cornmeal
1 tbsp. double acting baking
   powder
scant tsp. salt

²/₃ cup diced sharp
   Cheddar cheese
½ cup milk
pinch of ground caraway
1 tbsp. butter

Sift together flour, cornmeal, baking powder, and salt. Add cold butter cut into small pieces and blend gently until the mixture is crumbly. Add cheese, milk and caraway; mix until the mixture forms a dough. Roll out on a floured board, about ½ inch thick, cut 1½-inch circles, put on buttered baking sheet and bake at 400° for about 12 minutes until the biscuits are puffed up and golden brown.

Rolled Anchovy Cheese Sticks

18 slices white bread
4 oz. cream cheese
3 tbsp. heavy cream
1 tsp. capers, minced

pepper to taste
18 anchovy filets
4 tbsp. melted butter

Pare crust off thinly sliced bread. Place bread slices on a damp towel, cover with wax paper and roll them with a rolling pin to half their thickness. Blend well cream cheese, heavy cream, capers, pepper, spread on the flattened bread slices. Put an anchovy filet in the center of each slice and roll them up like a jelly roll. Place them on a baking sheet, brush with melted butter, bake in 450⁰ oven for a few minutes until well browned. Serve piping hot.

Cooked Cheese

(for 4 to 6)

1 lb. farmer cheese
salt to taste
1 tsp. crushed caraway seeds

1 tsp. paprika
1 cup butter
2 egg yolks, lightly beaten

Put a layer of cheese in a glass dish, sprinkle with some salt, caraway and paprika; add several more layers of cheese sprinkled with salt, caraway and paprika. Cover the dish and let stand in a cool place — not refrigerated — for 2 or 3 days. By that time the cheese will be slightly runny.

Melt butter in a saucepan, add cheese and stir constantly over low heat until well blended and the cheese has melted. Add egg yolks, blend for another minute. Pour mixture in a crock or bowl and chill well. For serving, unmold and slice.

Endives a la Suisse

(for 4)

4 large heads Belgian Endives   butter
    (or 8 small heads)   4 tbsp. sour cream
4 slices Swiss cheese,   salt and pepper to taste
    ⅛ -inch thick

Wash endives, place in slightly salted boiling water, cover and cook for 7 to 8 minutes. Do not overcook. Drain well and cool. Wrap a slice of cheese around each endive so, if small endives were used, wrap two in a slice of cheese. Place them in a well-buttered baking dish or casserole, top with sour cream, season with salt and pepper. Bake at 375⁰ for about 10 minutes.

Roquefort Endives

(for 6)

12 average size endives
1 cup chicken broth
  (or 1 cup water and 2
  chicken bouillon cubes)

3 tbsp. butter
salt and pepper to taste
8 oz. Roquefort cheese

Wash endives in cold water, trim off any withered leaves. Split them lengthwise in half. Place endives in a saucepan, add chicken broth or water and bouillon cubes. Simmer until endives have slightly softened — about 15 minutes. Remove carefully with a spatula or slotted spoon, drain and place in shallow baking dish. Dot with butter, season with salt and pepper. Crumble cheese all over the top, place under a medium broiler for about 3 minutes or until nicely browned.

Cheese Chili
(for 4)

½ cup minced onion
½ small clove garlic,
    minced
½ tbsp. oil
1 cup canned tomatoes,
    drained
½ cup light cream

salt and pepper to taste
2 tsp. chili powder
pinch of Cayenne pepper
1 cup grated sharp
    Cheddar cheese
3 eggs, lightly beaten

Sauté onions in oil until limp and lightly browned, add garlic, tomatoes, cream, salt, pepper, chili powder and Cayenne, cover and simmer very gently for 15 minutes. Stir in the cheese, cook while stirring until melted, then stir in the eggs. Cook while stirring constantly until the mixture has thickened. Do not let boil.

Swiss Custard

(for 4)

4 slices smoked bacon
2 eggs
½ cup ale
½ cup heavy cream
¼ cup minced cooked ham

1 tbsp. minced onion
¾ cup grated Gruyere
  or Swiss cheese
¼ cup grated Romano cheese
salt and pepper to taste

Fry bacon until well browned, drain on paper towel and crumble. Blend eggs, ale and cream, beat well; add crumbled bacon, ham, onion, both cheeses, season with salt and pepper. Pour mixture into individual custard cups, set them in a pan half filled with hot water, bake at 425° for about 15 to 20 minutes. When a knife inserted in the center comes out clean, the custard is done.

Cheese Dumplings

1 lb. pot cheese or
  farmer cheese
4 eggs, separated
3 tbsp. butter, softened
½ cup farina
pinch of salt

2 tbsp. flour
1 tbsp. salt
½ cup breadcrumbs
4 tbsp. butter
confectioner's sugar

Rub cheese through a strainer. Blend with beaten egg yolks, softened butter, farina, pinch of salt and flour. Fold in stiffly beaten egg whites, let stand for half an hour.

Bring water to a boil in a large saucepan, add 1 tablespoon salt. Take a tablespoon of the cheese mixture, shape it into a ball and drop it in the boiling water. Cook for 10 minutes. Test for doneness. If dumpling is too light and falls apart, add more farina to the mixture, if too heavy, a spoonful of sour cream.

When dumplings are cooked, drain them well. Heat remaining butter, sauté breadcrumbs until golden brown, roll dumplings in the mixture and sprinkle with ample sugar when serving.

Cheese Blintzes

(about 16 blintzes)

Batter:
4 eggs, well beaten
1 cup milk
½ tsp. salt
1 cup flour
1 tbsp. melted butter

Filling:
1 lb. cottage cheese, riced
   or rubbed through a
   strainer
2 egg yolks, beaten
3 tbsp. sugar
1 tbsp. sour cream
½ tsp. vanilla extract
¼ tsp. cinnamon
butter for frying

To make the batter, add milk and salt to beaten eggs, blend well, add flour gradually while stirring, then the melted butter. Blend until smooth.

Combine all ingredients for the filling. Heat a well greased heavy 6-inch skillet and pour in just enough batter to make a thin pancake. Tilt the skillet to cover the bottom evenly with the batter. As soon as the underside is lightly browned, turn out on a board, browned side up. Grease the pan again, cook the next blintze and so on. When the desired number have been cooked, pat a portion of the filling on each of the browned sides, fold two sides over the center, then the other two sides, to form an envelope. Just before serving, fry in hot butter until nicely browned on both sides.

Serve with stewed fruit, or with sour cream and fresh berries, or sprinkle with sugar and cinnamon.

Fried Cheese

1 egg white, stiffly beaten
2 cups grated Parmesan
   or Romano cheese

1 tbsp. minced parsley
oil for frying

Combine 1 cup grated cheese, half of the beaten egg white and ½ tablespoon parsley, heat and blend well. Add remaining egg white, cheese and parsley, a little at a time, while beating. Shape into small balls, fry quickly in hot oil until golden. Drain on paper towel, serve very hot.

Fried Cheese Slices

small pieces of feta
   cheese, cut ¼-inch thick

butter
lemon juice

Heat butter in a skillet, brown cheese pieces on both sides, sprinkle with lemon juice when serving.

Fried Cheese Sandwich

(for 6)

12 slices firm white
  bread, crust removed
½ cup flour
3 eggs, lightly beaten
  with 2 tbsp. milk

salt and pepper to taste
½ cup oil
¾ lb. Mozarella cheese,
  sliced thin

Cover 6 slices of bread with cheese, season with salt and pepper, cover with remaining bread to make 6 sandwiches. Cut each sandwich diagonally in half, dip in beaten eggs, then in flour and then in eggs again.

Heat oil in a skillet, fry sandwiches until nicely browned on both sides.

Greek Cheese Pie

(for 6)

3 eggs, well beaten
1 lb. feta cheese
pepper to taste
3 tbsp. softened butter

2 tbsp. parsley, chopped
2 tbsp. dill, chopped
½ lb. phyllo pastry sheets
melted butter

Crumble cheese and mash with a fork. Blend with eggs, pepper and softened butter. Mix in parsley and dill. Place a sheet of phyllo pastry in a pan about the size of the sheet, butter the sheet, place another sheet on top, butter again and continue for a total of 8 sheets. Spread the cheese mixture on top and cover with 8 more buttered phyllo sheets. Bake in 350^0 oven for about 30 minutes until golden brown. Cut into squares and serve warm.

Note: Phyllo pastry sheets can be bought in all stores selling Greek or Mid-Eastern foods. They are also carried by many supermarkets.

Cheese and Potato Casserole

(for 4 to 6)

2 cups cottage cheese
½ cup sour cream
2½ cups mashed boiled
   potatoes, riced
3 tbsp. butter, melted
salt and pepper to taste

2 tbsp. grated onion
2 tbsp. minced parsley
2 tbsp. chopped olives
2 tbsp. butter
paprika

Beat cheese with a wire whisk until smooth. Rub through a strainer, blend with sour cream. Add riced potatoes while they are still warm, combine well with cheese and all other ingredients, except 2 tablespoons butter. Butter a 9-inch pie plate or baking dish, fill with the mixture, dot with butter, sprinkle with paprika. Bake at 350° for about 45 minutes until top is nicely browned.

Cheese Straws

2 cups sifted flour
2 cups grated Cheddar cheese,
   (or 1½ cups Cheddar
   and ½ cup Parmesan)
1 tsp. salt
1½ tbsp. butter
cold milk
ice water

Blend flour with cheese, salt and softened butter. Gradually add half milk and half ice water, just enough to make a stiff dough. Roll out ¼-inch thick. Cut in strips ¼-inch wide and about 4 to 5 inches long. Put on a baking sheet and bake at 400⁰ for about 10 minutes until golden brown.

Cheese Toast Savoy
(for 4)

½ lb. shredded Swiss
   cheese
¼ cup dry white wine
3 anchovy filets, mashed
1 egg, lightly beaten
1 tbsp. pitted olives,
   chopped
1 tsp. pimiento, chopped
salt and pepper to taste
toasted English muffins

Put cheese and wine in a saucepan, melt over low heat and blend well, until thick and creamy. Add anchovy filets, egg, olives and pimiento, stir until well blended. Spread toasted muffins with the mixture, place them on a baking sheet and brown in a hot oven or under the broiler.

Cheese Puffs

(for 6)

½ cup butter
1 cup water
½ tsp. salt
pinch of sugar

1¾ cups flour
6 eggs
⅓ lb. Swiss cheese, grated
fat for deep frying

Heat butter in a saucepan, add water, salt and sugar. Bring the mixture to the boiling point, add the flour all at once and stir vigorously with a wooden spoon until the mixture clears the sides of the saucepan.

Remove from heat and beat in the eggs, one at a time, beating well after each addition. Then beat in the grated cheese. The dough should be smooth and shiny.

Heat the frying fat to 375°. Drop in the batter by the tablespoon. Fry the puffs until they are golden and have turned upside down. Fry only a few at a time. They should not be crowded.

Remove the puffs with a skimmer or slotted spoon, drain them on a paper towel and put them on a hot serving dish lined with a napkin. Keep hot until all are done.

Cheesecake
(for 8)

For the crust:
1 cup fine cracker crumbs
  (Graham crackers, cookies
  or zwieback)
4 tbsp. melted butter
pinch of cinnamon

For the topping:
1 cup sour cream
2 tbsp. sugar
½ tsp. vanilla

For the filling:
1 lb. cream cheese at
  room temperature
1 lb. farmer cheese
¾ cup sugar
2 eggs, beaten
¾ cup sour cream
⅓ cup milk
1 tsp. vanilla
3 tbsp. flour
pinch of salt

Mix the cracker crumbs and the butter, add cinnamon and blend well. Pat into a well greased spring form pan.

Combine and blend the cheeses with a hand or electric mixer, beat in sugar and eggs until smooth, then all other ingredients. Pour this batter in the pan lined with the crust, bake in a preheated 350⁰ oven for 30 minutes or until the center of the cake is fairly firm. Remove from oven and cool the cake.

Mix the topping ingredients and spread on the cake. Heat oven to 450⁰ and bake 4 minutes longer. The topping will set as the cake cools.

Finnish Cheese Cake

(for 6)

2 cups cottage cheese
¼ cup flour
3 eggs, lightly beaten
⅓ cup sugar
2 cups light cream
1 tbsp. butter

½ cup toasted almonds,
    chopped
¼ cup candied fruit,
    chopped
2 tbsp. brandy

Stir cottage cheese in a bowl until lumps are broken up. Add flour, mix well, add all other ingredients except butter, blend until smooth. Pour mixture in a buttered 8-inch baking dish or pie plate, bake at 350⁰ for about 1 hour or until the cake is set and a knife inserted in the center comes out clean.

Coeur à la Creme

(for 6)

1 lb. cream cheese
1¼ cups heavy cream
pinch of salt

2 egg whites, beaten
    stiff

Rub cream cheese through a strainer, blend well with heavy cream and salt and beat with a wooden spoon until smooth. Fold in beaten egg whites. Line a heart-shaped wicker basket or individual Coeur à la Creme molds with cheesecloth, spoon the mixture into the molds. Place the mold in a pan to catch the draining juices and refrigerate for at least 12 hours until well drained and firm. Unmold on a serving plate and surround with fresh strawberries, raspberries or other fresh fruit in season.

Floating Island

(for 4)

1¾ cups milk
¼ cup sugar
¼ tsp. salt
3 eggs
1 egg, separated

1 tbsp. orange juice concentrate
½ tsp. grated lemon peel
½ tsp. lemon juice
⅛ tsp. cream of tartar
2 tbsp. sugar

In small mixing bowl beat the egg white and cream of tartar until foamy. Add 2 tablespoons sugar, 1 tablespoon at a time, beating constantly until sugar is dissolved* and white is glossy and stands in soft peaks. In small skillet or large heavy saucepan heat milk over low heat until simmering. Drop 4 meringues, using about ⅓ cup each, onto milk. Simmer, uncovered, until firm, about 5 minutes. Using slotted spoon lift meringue from milk, onto paper toweling to drain. Reserve milk for custard. Chill meringues while preparing custard. In same or medium saucepan beat eggs and egg yolk with ¼ cup sugar and salt. Gradually pour reserved warm milk into egg mixture, stirring until blended. Cook and stir over low heat until mixture thickens slightly and just coats a metal spoon. Remove from heat. Stir in orange juice concentrate and lemon extract. Pour into 1-quart shallow serving dish, 9-inch pie plate or 4 (9-ounce) custard cups. Top custard with meringues. Chill.

*Rub just a bit of meringue between thumb and forefinger to feel if sugar is dissolved.

Floating Island.

Custard with Sparkling Wine Sauce

(for 6)

Custard:

6 eggs
$^1/_3$ cup sugar
1 tsp. vanilla extract
pinch of salt
1½ cups light cream
1¾ cups milk

Sparkling Sauce:

1 pint fresh strawberries
3 tbsp. currant jelly
1 tsp. cornstarch
1 tbsp. water
2 tsp. sugar
$^1/_3$ to ½ cup sparkling wine

Custard: Beat together eggs, sugar, vanilla and salt. Stir in cream and milk. Pour into a buttered 5½ cup ring mold. Place mold in a pan of hot water. Bake in 350⁰ oven for 40 minutes or until knife inserted in center comes out clean. Unmold onto a serving plate and chill well until serving time.

Sparkling sauce: Purée 1 cup strawberries in a blender, strain. In a small saucepan melt jelly over low heat. Mix cornstarch and water, stir into the melted jelly, add sugar and half of the strawberry purée. Bring to a boil and cook while stirring for one minute. Remove from fire, stir in remaining purée and chill. At serving time, pour the sparkling wine into the strawberry sauce. Garnish custard with remaining strawberries and serve sauce on the side.

Creme Caramel—See recipe on p. 139.

Cottage Cheese Soufflé

(for 6)

½ cup butter
½ cup sugar
4 eggs, separated
½ lb. cottage cheese,
   rubbed through a sieve
⅓ cup seedless raisins

2 tbsp. candied citron,
   chopped
1 tsp. lemon juice
½ tsp. grated lemon rind
1 cup sour cream
½ tsp. cinnamon

Blend butter, sugar and egg yolks until smooth and creamy. Mix in cottage cheese, raisins, citron, lemon juice, lemon rind and sour cream, blend well. Fold in stiffly beaten egg whites. Pour mixture into a buttered baking or soufflé dish, sprinkle with cinnamon. Set dish in a pan half filled with hot water. Bake at 350⁰ for one hour.

Creme Caramel

(for 6)

1 cup sugar, divided	2 cups milk, heated
3 eggs	until very warm
3 egg yolks	1 tsp. vanilla

In heavy saucepan, over medium heat, melt ½ cup sugar, stirring constantly until a deep golden brown. Remove from heat and *immediately* pour about 1 tablespoon into each of six 6-ounce custard cups. Set aside. Mix eggs, egg yolks and remaining sugar together until well blended. Gradually stir in milk. Add vanilla. Pour into prepared custard cups over caramel. Set cups in large baking pan. Pour very hot water into pan to within ½ inch of top of custard. Bake in preheated 350°F. oven 45 to 50 minutes or until knife inserted near center comes out clean. Remove promptly from hot water. To serve warm: Cool 5 to 10 minutes at room temperature. Gently loosen custard from cups at sides with spatula and invert on serving plate. To serve cold: Chill in refrigerator and unmold.

Flan

⅓ cup light brown sugar	6 tbsp. rum (opt.)
3 cups milk	pinch of salt
scant ½ cup sugar	1 tsp. vanilla extract
	6 eggs

Put brown sugar in a pan the flan is to be baked in, melt sugar over moderate heat and stir until sugar starts to turn a deeper brown. Swirl the pan to cover the entire surface with the melted sugar. Remove pan from heat. Beat the eggs until creamy, beat in sugar, then add salt, milk and vanilla, blend well. Pour the mixture into the caramel lined pan, set the pan in a slightly larger one, half filled with hot water. Bake in 350° oven for about half an hour or more until the tip of a knife inserted in the custard comes out clean. Remove pan from the oven and waterbath, cool. When cool, loosen the edges of the custard with a knife or spatula, place a serving dish on top, invert quickly.

Before serving, pour warmed rum over the flan and ignite.

Pashka
Russian Easter Dessert
(for 6 to 8)

1 lb. cream cheese
½ cup sour cream
½ cup butter
1 cup powdered sugar
¼ tsp. vanilla extract
¼ tsp. almond extract
1 tsp. grated lemon rind

1 cup seedless raisins
4 oz. mixed candied
   fruit
¾ cup blanched almonds
¼ tsp. salt
candied cherries

Blend cream cheese with sour cream and softened butter and beat until smooth. Soak raisins in hot water until soft and plumped. Chop the almonds and mixed candied fruit. Add, together with all other ingredients, except the candied cherries, to cheese mixture. Mix and beat until well blended and smooth. The mixture should be fairly firm, add more cream cheese and sugar if too soft. Line a clean flower pot or a perforated mold with muslin or triple cheesecloth, fill with the cheese mixture, cover and place a weight on top. Stand on a wire rack, put in a cool place and let drain for 12 hours. Turn the pashka out on a platter, decorate with candied cherries.

Ricotta Pie

(for 6)

2 cups flour	$^1/_3$ cup sugar
pinch of salt	$^1/_2$ tsp. vanilla extract
$^2/_3$ cup butter	$^1/_2$ tsp. almond extract
2 tbsp. sherry	2 tbsp. dark rum
1$^1/_2$ lbs. Ricotta cheese	4 tbsp. chopped blanched almonds
4 eggs	2 tbsp. chopped candied citron

Sift together flour and salt into a bowl. Cut in butter and add sherry. Mix gently and add a little water if needed to hold the dough together. Roll out $^1/_8$-inch thick. Line a 10-inch buttered pie plate with the dough, use the remaining dough to cut $^1/_2$-inch wide strips for lattice to cover the pie.

Rub Ricotta cheese through a sieve. Beat eggs and sugar until light and foamy, add vanilla, almond extract and rum, add to cheese, also almonds and citron and whisk until well blended. Pour mixture in the pie shell, place dough strips over the top and pinch the edges together. Bake at 350° for about 45 minutes until the center is firm and the dough golden brown. Cool before serving.

Basic Dessert Omelette

(for 2 to 3)

5 eggs   2 tbsp. sugar
2 tbsp. rum or Kirsch   ¼ cup butter

Break the eggs into a bowl and beat them with a wire whisk until they are frothy. Beating constantly, add rum or Kirsch and sugar.

Heat butter in an omelette pan or skillet until it stops foaming and is pale gold. Pour in the eggs and make the omelette in the usual manner. Turn half the omelette over the other half and let it stand for 2 minutes over very low heat. Turn it onto a serving dish and serve immediately.

Rum Omelette

(for 4)

6 eggs, separated   ½ tsp. vanilla extract
½ cup sugar   pinch of salt
1 tbsp. butter   ⅓ cup strawberry preserve
¼ cup rum

Beat the egg yolks until creamy, blend in sugar, rum, vanilla and salt. Beat egg whites stiff, fold into the yolk mixture. Heat butter in a skillet or omelette pan and cook the omelette in the usual manner over low heat. When done, spread omelette with strawberry preserve, fold over and serve.

Apricot Omelette Soufflé

(for 4 to 6)

8 eggs, separated
2 tbsp. sugar
2 tbsp. white wine
  (or water)
pinch of salt

2 tbsp. butter
½ cup apricot preserve
confectioner's sugar
3 tbsp. Kirsch brandy
  or light rum

Beat egg yolks with 2 tablespoons sugar, salt and wine until frothy. Fold in the stiffly beaten egg whites. Heat butter in a large skillet or omelette pan, cover the entire bottom with melted butter, pour in egg mixture. Cook very slowly until the bottom is brown and the omelette puffed up. Bake in a 450⁰ oven for 3 or 4 minutes to finish cooking the top without browning it.

Remove from oven, spread with apricot preserve, fold the omelette and turn it out on a hot serving plate. Sprinkle with sugar, pour Kirsch around it and ignite.

Ricotta Flambé

(for 6)

1½ lbs. Ricotta cheese
¼ cup milk
3 tbsp. sugar (or to
   taste)

6 tbsp. brandy
2 tbsp. semi-sweet chocolate
   grated

Blend Ricotta with milk, sugar and 3 tablespoons brandy, beat until smooth and creamy. Put into a serving bowl and chill for 2 or 3 hours. Just before serving, heat the remaining brandy, pour over the cheese and ignite. Spoon Ricotta into serving cups and sprinkle with grated chocolate.

Frozen Egg Nog
(for 6)

3 egg yolks
⅔ cup powdered sugar
¼ cup Cognac brandy
3 tbsp. Grand Marnier
   or Benedictine liqueur

¼ tsp. mace
3 egg whites, stiffly
   beaten
2 cups heavy cream,
   whipped

    Beat yolks until light and frothy. Whisk in sugar, Cognac and Grand Marnier, fold in mace, egg whites and whipped cream. Spoon mixture into freezing trays, place in freezer. When partially frozen, stir well, fill into a mold and freeze.

Frozen Sabayon

(for 4)

3 large egg yolks

2 tbsp. water

3 tbsp. sugar

⅛ tsp. grated nutmeg

½ cup Marsala wine

3 tbsp. dark rum

1 cup heavy cream,
  whipped

Put all ingredients except cream in top of double boiler. The water in the bottom part should be simmering, not boiling. Blend mixture with a wire whisk until the mixture is warm. Remove from heat and continue whisking until the mixture is frothy and slightly thickened. Cool, then fold in whipped cream. Pour mixture into a mold or serving bowl and freeze. If a mold is used, dip it just before serving for a second or two in hot water, cover with a serving dish and invert.

Salzburg Soufflé
(for 4)

⅓ cup butter
8 eggs, separated
3 tbsp. flour
½ tsp. vanilla extract

½ cup sugar
¼ cup hot milk
confectioner's sugar

Cream butter, add egg yolks and flour and beat until light and fluffy. Beat egg whites very stiff, gradually adding sugar and vanilla while beating. The success in making the soufflé depends largely on the stiffness of the egg whites. Fold egg whites into the yolks. Pour milk in a baking dish, pour in egg mixture and bake in a pre-heated 350⁰ oven for 10 minutes until top is lightly browned. Remove from pan in big spoonfuls to a serving dish, dust with sugar and serve.

Note: The mixture should stand in the baking pan about 1-inch deep before cooking.

Cherry Pancake
(for 2)

1 cup flour
½ cup plus 1 tbsp. milk
4 eggs, separated
pinch of salt
¼ cup sugar

½ tsp. lemon juice
3 tbsp. melted butter
1 cup pitted cherries
4 tbsp. butter
confectioner's sugar

Mix flour and milk until smooth. Blend in beaten egg yolks, salt, sugar, lemon juice and melted butter. Just before cooking fold in beaten egg whites and cherries. Heat some of the remaining butter in a skillet. Pour batter in — about 1 inch high. Cook one side until light golden, turn and cook the other side. Tear in small pieces with a fork and continue cooking for half a minute. Remove from skillet, keep warm. Make more pancakes until all the batter is used up, sprinkle with sugar before serving.

Note: A tablespoon or two of rum may be added to the batter before cooking.

Viennese Pancakes

(for 6)

For the pancakes:

1 ¼ cups flour

2 eggs

½ cup water

¾ cup milk

1 tbsp. sugar

pinch of salt

3 tbsp. butter

Sift flour with salt into a bowl. Stir in eggs, milk, water and sugar, blend well to make a smooth pancake batter. Heat an 8-inch skillet and add just enough butter to cover the surface. Ladle some batter into the skillet and cover the bottom thinly by tilting and twisting the skillet. Cook until the top of the batter bubbles, turn the pancake and quickly brown the other side for just a few seconds. Slide pancake on a warm plate and repeat until all the batter is used up, adding butter to the skillet before cooking each pancake.

The Filling:

½ cup butter

¾ cup sugar

2 whole eggs

2 egg yolks

3 tbsp. raisins

1 cup cottage or farmer
cheese rubbed through
a strainer

4 tbsp. sour cream

confectioner's sugar

Cream the butter, add sugar and eggs, one at a time, while beating the mixture. Add egg yolks, cheese, raisins and sour cream, blend well. Spread each pancake with some of the mixture, roll them up and place them side by side in a buttered baking dish. Bake at 350⁰ for 10 to 15 minutes. Sprinkle with sugar before serving.

Zabaglione

(for 4)

4 egg yolks
¾ cup sugar

¾ cup Marsala wine
¼ tsp. grated nutmeg

Beat egg yolks lightly, put with all other ingredients in the top of a double boiler. The water in the bottom part should be simmering but not boiling. Beat mixture with a wire whisk until mixture is very thick and foamy. Serve immediately in parfait glasses or other long-stemmed glasses. If you want to serve a cold Zabaglione, you can prepare this dessert in advance. Cook Zabaglione as above, then set the top of the double boiler containing the mixture in a pot filled with cracked ice. Continue beating with the whisk until the mixture is very cold, otherwise the Zabaglione will separate. Fill serving glasses and refrigerate.

Zabaglione Sauce

(about 3 cups)

3 egg yolks
1⅓ cups sugar
pinch of grated nutmeg

1¾ cups Marsala wine
¾ cup heavy cream,
  whipped

Beat egg yolks until creamy, put in top of a double boiler, mix in sugar, nutmeg and Marsala. Place over simmering water and beat with a rotary hand beater or wire whisk until the mixture thickens and is creamy. Remove from fire and continue beating until the mixture is cool. Fold in whipped cream, serve with cooked fruit, marinated strawberries, peaches, etc.

Sauce Bechamel

3 tbsp. butter
1 tbsp. onion, minced
4 tbsp. flour
3 cups scalded milk

salt and white pepper
 to taste
pinch of grated nutmeg

Melt butter in a saucepan, add onion and sauté while stirring for a few minutes until onion is soft, but not browned. Stir in flour and cook, while stirring, until the flour just starts to take on color. Gradually add the scalded milk, stir with a whisk until the mixture is smooth and has thickened. Season with salt, pepper and nutmeg. Strain before using.

Sauce Mornay

2 cups hot Sauce
 Bechamel
2 lightly beaten egg
 yolks

½ cup grated Gruyere
 or Swiss cheese
dash of Tabasco sauce
 (opt.)

Combine egg yolks with a few spoonfuls of Bechamel, then add to the rest of the Bechamel sauce. Blend well, season with Tabasco sauce. Bring to a simmer but do not let boil. Simmer for a minute or two stir in the cheese and simmer while stirring until the cheese has melted and the sauce is smooth. Correct seasoning.

Chive Sauce

(for 4)

4 hard-boiled eggs
1½ tbsp. oil
1½ tbsp. vinegar
2½ tbsp. chives, minced

salt and pepper to taste
1 tsp. sugar (or to taste)
water

Rub egg yolks through a strainer into a bowl, combine with vinegar and just enough water to make a sauce the consistency of mayonnaise. Rub egg whites through the strainer into the sauce, add all other ingredients and blend well. Add more water and vinegar to taste, to make the sauce the consistency of a very thin mayonnaise.

This sauce is excellent served with boiled meats, poached fish or cold meats.

Sauce Gribiche
(about 1 cup)

3 hard-boiled eggs
salt and pepper to taste
1 tsp. Dijon mustard
1½ cups olive oil
½ cup white wine
   vinegar

2 tbsp. minced sour gherkins
   (cornichons)
2 tbsp. drained, chopped capers
1 tbsp. minced parsley
1 tbsp. minced chives
½ tsp. dried tarragon

Rub egg yolks through a strainer, add salt, pepper, mustard and stir until smooth. Blend in 2 tablespoons vinegar, start adding oil while beating or whisking, a little at a time at first, as if making a regular mayonnaise, then in a thin stream. Alternate with a little vinegar and continue beating until oil and vinegar are used up. Rub egg whites through a coarse strainer and blend in together with all other ingredients.

Excellent with cold fish, shellfish and vegetables.

Sauce Hollandaise

¼ cup white wine vinegar
½ lb. butter
3 egg yolks, lightly
    beaten

2 tbsp. water
salt and white pepper
    to taste

Place vinegar in the top half of a double boiler, put directly over low heat and cook until the vinegar has been reduced to about ½ teaspoon. Remove from fire and cool.

Melt butter very slowly in a saucepan, decant into a measuring cup and discard the milky sediment in the bottom of the pan. Add egg yolks and water to the vinegar in the top of the double boiler, place over barely simmering water and beat with a wire whisk until light and frothy. Slowly add the melted butter to the eggs, a little at a time, beating constantly with the whisk, until the sauce is smooth and thick. Season with salt and pepper and serve at once.

You can keep the Hollandaise over warm but not boiling water for half an hour or so — kept longer the sauce deteriorates.

Egg and Lemon Sauce

(about 1 cup)

3 eggs, separated
salt and white pepper
   to taste

juice of 2 small
   lemons
1 cup hot chicken broth

Beat egg whites until fairly stiff but not dry. Beat in egg yolks, one at a time. Add slowly, while beating, lemon juice and the hot broth, a spoonful at a time. It is important to add the ingredients quite slowly to avoid curdling. When smooth, season with salt and pepper.

This sauce is used in gravies and stews or fricassees. Add the mixture slowly to hot sauce or stew, beating constantly until the sauce thickens.

Green Mayonnaise

(about 1¼ cups)

1 cup mayonnaise
2 tbsp. parsley
2 tbsp. fresh dill or
   tarragon
2 tbsp. chives

3 tbsp. spinach
2 tbsp. watercress
2 hard-boiled egg yolks
salt and pepper to taste

In a small saucepan, bring 1 cup water to a boil, add herbs and vegetables, blanch for 2 minutes, drain well and chop very fine. Rub through a strainer, also the hard-boiled egg yolks; blend with mayonnaise and correct seasoning. Serve with cold seafood, fish and vegetables.

Roquefort Sauce

$^1/_3$ cup Roquefort cheese,
   crumbled
1 small clove garlic,
   minced
1 raw egg yolk
1 hard-boiled egg, rubbed
   through a strainer
5 tbsp. olive oil

5 tbsp. corn oil
2 tbsp. white wine vinegar
1 tbsp. lemon juice
1 tsp. grated onion
1½ tsp. Dijon mustard
salt and pepper to taste
pinch of powdered cardamom
1 tsp. sugar

Blend all ingredients in a blender or with a rotary beater. Store refrigerated. Serve with hard-boiled eggs, other egg dishes and salads.

Roquefort-Anchovy Sauce

(about 1½ cups)

$^2/_3$ cup Roquefort or blue
   cheese, crumbled
$^2/_3$ cup olive oil
1 small can of anchovies
   (with the oil)
4 tbsp. vinegar
2 tbsp. lemon juice
pepper to taste

1 small clove garlic,
   minced
½ tsp. paprika
1 tsp. prepared horseradish
½ tsp. Dijon mustard
1 tsp. sugar
½ tsp. A-1 sauce
pinch of Cayenne pepper

Place all ingredients in a food processor or blender, blend thoroughly. Use as a salad dressing or with cold meats or cooked chilled vegetables.

Sauce Remoulade
(about 1¼ cups)

1 cup mayonnaise
1 tbsp. minced sour pickles
   (cornichons)
1 tbsp. drained, chopped
   capers
1 tbsp. Dijon mustard

1 tbsp. minced parsley
1 tsp. minced chives
1 tsp. minced fresh tarragon
   (½ tsp. dried)
½ tsp. dried chervil
1 anchovy filet, mashed

Combine all ingredients and mix until well blended. Serve with cold fish or meats.

Sauce Tartare
(1¼ cups)

1 cup mayonnaise
1 tsp. Dijon mustard
1 tsp. minced shallots
1 tbsp. minced gherkins
1 tbsp. drained capers,
   chopped
1 tsp. minced parsley

½ tsp. sugar
½ tsp. anchovy paste
1 hard-boiled egg, minced
1 tbsp. chopped green olives
1½ tsp. white wine vinegar
   (or to taste)
salt and pepper to taste

Blend all ingredients until well combined. Serve with fried seafood, fried egg dishes and others.

Index